YEAH BUT NO BUT

YEAH BUT NO BUT

THE BIOGRAPHY OF MATT LUCAS AND DAVID WALLIAMS

NEIL SIMPSON

JOHN BLAKE

Published by John Blake Publishing Ltd,
3 Bramber Court, 2 Bramber Road,
London W14 9PB, England

www.blake.co.uk

First published in hardback in 2006

ISBN 1 84454 258 0

British Library Cataloguing-in-Publication Data:

A catalogue record for this book is available from the British Library.

Design by www.envydesign.co.uk

Printed in Great Britain by Creative Print and Design, Wales

3 5 7 9 10 8 6 4 2

Papers used by John Blake Publishing are natural, recyclable products made
from wood grown in sustainable forests. The manufacturing processes conform
to the environmental regulations of the country of origin.

Every attempt has been made to contact the relevant copyright-holders,
but some were unobtainable. We would be grateful if the appropriate people
could contact us.

CONTENTS

CHAPTER 1

OPENING NIGHT

The curtain was due to rise in less than an hour and the ticket touts were getting frantic. People were crowding around them, all prepared to pay up to five times the £25 face value of any tickets they had on offer. But almost all the touts were empty handed. No one who had a ticket was selling, and tempers were getting strained.

'Tickets? Come on – anybody got any tickets?'

The touts did one more sweep of the crowd outside Portsmouth's 2,200-seater Guildhall Theatre. Surely someone, somewhere, was prepared to take the cash and give the show a miss? It didn't seem as if they were. For this was 25 October 2005, the first night of the first ever *Little Britain* live tour. And the show was already a theatrical phenomenon.

The original 100-date nationwide tour had been announced more than six months earlier and 150,000 tickets had been sold within the first six hours of release. The final batch of 50,000 tickets had been snapped up by the end of that first day and within a month dozens of extra dates had been added. When these sold out and the London dates were announced for the autumn of 2006, the phones rang off the hook as the central box office once more struggled to meet demand.

In Portsmouth, everyone knew that the opening night wasn't just the hottest ticket in town – it was the hottest ticket in the country. Television crews were filming the crowds, and critics from every national newspaper had headed down from London to report on the action. The sense of anticipation and excitement was palpable. And inside the theatre the show's stars were feeling the heat.

'Are we ready for this?' Matt and David were sitting in make-up as the audience began to take its seats. And if they had poked their heads round from behind the fire curtain they might well have felt as though they were looking in a mirror. There were several bulky men badly dressed as women, some with parasols and lace gloves. Other younger men had squeezed into tight red PVC suits. Then there were the middle-aged women dressed in teenage-style shell suits with scrunched-up hair and plenty of eye make-up. As the pictures in the next day's newspapers would attest, fans of *Little Britain* would go to amazing lengths to look like their favourite comedy characters – characters who had become national institutions and extraordinary cash generators in less than five short years.

For Matt and David, the whole experience still seemed unbelievable – in many ways it was as surreal as many of their most extraordinary sketches. This was to be the first time they had done a regular stage act together in nearly eight years. And the contrasts between that previous occasion and this one could hardly be greater. Back then they had been at the very bottom of the comedy pile, performing as the fictional thespian and raconteur Sir Bernard Chumley and his deeply disturbing sidekick Anthony Rogers (their unspoken joke had been 'Anthony rogers who?').

That act had endured the indignities of the very latest and least attractive slots at the Edinburgh Festival. Afterwards, they had slogged it out on the fractured comedy circuit in London, where audiences could be brutal and indifferent in equal measure. On one occasion, when the duo were supposedly headlining in a north London community centre that could seat 150 people, the theatre manager had asked the single-figure audience if they minded delaying the show's start by half an hour. 'A few more people might turn up when *EastEnders* finishes,' he had said hopefully. The audience was happy to go back to the bar and wait, but the theatre manager turned out to be wrong. No one else did turn up and when the show finally began there were almost as many people off stage as on.

Portsmouth in 2005 was an entirely different world. Director Jeremy Sams, set designer Andrew Howe-Davies and stage manager Gareth Weeks led a near 50-strong team and had spent some £2 million putting together a massive high-tech show with two hours' worth of computer-generated backdrops and settings, pre-recorded voice-overs and music. And the show was to begin with a big set-piece scene that the stars could only have dreamed about a decade earlier. Matt and David had decided to open the show with a Lou and Andy sketch – and, as the lights went down, David's Lou was due to walk around the audience searching for his supposedly wheelchair-bound charge Andy. As the search went on, Matt, as Andy, was to fly across the stage on an invisible high wire before landing in his wheelchair. It was a complicated, expensive sketch that would drive the audience wild night after night. But in the early evening of 25 October in Portsmouth, no one yet knew that it would work. Despite all the rehearsals, no one was quite sure if they could pull it off. So everyone was nervous.

Before heading into the spotlights, Matt and David felt the familiar strains and symptoms that had dogged them ever since their first stand-up performances some 13 years earlier. Matt says he always feels a sense of immense tiredness immediately before the start of a show. David's stage fright comes through in a feeling of near overwhelming nausea – though both say the demons are banished as soon as they feel the stage lights on their faces. And, fortunately, that was exactly what was going to happen when the curtain finally rose on the 2005 tour.

'You could tell that they were both nervous that first moment when they both got on stage together at the start of that first sketch and gave each other a quick smile that wasn't in the act,' says *Little Britain* super-fan Martin

Davies, who was sitting in the seventh row and had been bombarding the BBC's website for more than a year demanding a live show. 'But the reaction from the audience made it obvious that they were going to be OK and from then on I think they were able to enjoy themselves almost as much as I was.'

And Martin wasn't alone. One early problem the producers and director soon discovered they would have to tweak for future shows was allowing long enough breaks and pauses for laughter and applause – in rehearsals, the team had underestimated just how funny they were all going to be.

In many ways, everyone had been right to be cautious. It was true that in the autumn of 2005 *Little Britain* was a television and cultural phenomenon. It had won awards in the UK and around the world and was being shown everywhere from Israel to Russia. It was credited with single-handedly saving the BBC's troubled digital station BBC3. It accounted for a huge chunk of the profits of the corporation's commercial arm, BBC Worldwide. Its catchphrases were heard in school playgrounds, offices, factories and even nursing homes. Even its scripts had become hardback best-sellers and it had won comedy awards around the globe.

But though the show and its two stars had already made the transition from stand-up to radio and on to television, the entertainment industry is littered with examples of small-screen shows that failed the final hurdle of going live. In recent years, Rik Mayall and

Adrian Edmondson had created a stage hit with *Bottom*, but many other transfers had ended up falling flat.

'There is a huge difference between making a television show, and focusing everything on cameras and close-ups, and commanding a stage in a huge auditorium, where the audience at the back can be more than 200 yards away from you,' says director Ken Patterson. 'It is a different mindset, it requires a different performance and in many ways it needs entirely new material. People don't pay big money just to see a copy of something they can watch at home. Expectations are high in live theatre and if it doesn't work out from the very start you'll know about it and you can find it hard to recover.'

As if to prove this point, the critics were not universal in their praise for the opening show in Portsmouth. Yes, they found plenty to rave about, and so there were plenty of wildly enthusiastic quotes to put on the advertisements for the following year's London tour. 'There wasn't a dry seat in the house – fans were wetting themselves with laughter,' was the boys' favourite line from the opening night review in the *Sun*, for example.

But elsewhere a few things seemed to rankle. Dominic Maxwell in *The Times* wrote that Matt clearly thrived on having a live audience to bounce off when he played Marjorie Dawes, the infamously cruel leader of the Fat Fighters group. But when the ad-libs were forgotten, Dominic said the basic sketch needed more work. 'Lucas comes true on his promise to an overweight female volunteer that: "It will be the most humiliating experience of your life," without adding enough wit to make it entirely forgivable,' he concluded.

Criticism for excessive cruelty and for shooting at easy targets has long since dogged the *Little Britain* comedians. It is criticism they have always managed to deflect in the past, and they would be forced to do so again before this tour ended. But at the end of that first night in Portsmouth they were simply interested in out-and-out celebration. They wanted to focus on the positives – and it turned out that there were plenty to choose from.

Top of the list was their ability to cope when things went wrong – as is always likely to happen in the early days of a live tour. It was only then, when the pressure was on, that the pair found the lessons they had learned in a decade's worth of low-budget stand-up shows still held true. Matt was able to heckle and ad-lib for as long as it took for a microphone to be fixed or for part of a set to be moved. David could make the audience roar with just a sideways glance while the technicians rushed to get the sound system ready for the next scene. It wasn't always a seamless performance in Portsmouth – as it wouldn't be over the next 100-plus dates. But everyone seemed to like it all the more when the performers were forced to think on their feet and provide something extra. 'We loved it because we were returning to what we used to do,' says David when asked about that first night. 'It can be terrifying, but we're never happier than when we're in front of a live audience.'

The show itself had also surpassed their expectations.

Matt and David both knew that they were treading a fine line with the content. Audiences would obviously want to see their favourite characters and scenes. But as Patterson had said, they also needed to feel they were getting something other than just a re-run of the latest DVD. So alongside some classic Daffyd, Emily Howard and Vicky Pollard moments they had decided to revive some of the older characters who hadn't been seen on screen for more than a year. The former kids' TV presenter Des Kaye was top of that list, as the men felt his desperation to get back into the public eye would work well in front of a live audience. Hypnotist Kenny Craig was up for a recall for the same reasons.

Other well-established characters were spiced up for the tour – with Matt baring all in his fat suit as Bubbles de Vere and David bringing the house down by doing the same, minus the fat suit, as Sebastian Love. The projectile-vomiting machine (full of a secret mix of porridge and lemonade) was in heavy use in the Maggie and Judy scenes, which drew almost as many laughs, even though everyone knew exactly what was going to happen from the moment Middle England's finest ambled on to the stage.

When writing the show's scripts, Matt and David had been particularly excited by the fact that, with a ticket-buying adult audience, they could push the boundaries of good taste and political correctness even further than they had been able to do on mainstream television. They also wanted the chance to road-test some new characters in advance of the third small-screen series, which was due to begin just after the tour.

The most popular of these turned out to be Mr Dudley, the sad, scruffy man with his £80 mail-order Thai bride Ting Tong Mackadandan. Matt and David had got the initial idea for 'Ting Tong from Ping Pong' after watching a Louis Theroux documentary about middle-aged western men who travelled to Thailand in search of young, docile wives. 'What if one day one of those men gets a shock?' they asked themselves in David's flash new north London kitchen, where they put together most of their scripts. 'What if one of the brides isn't quite as docile as she appears?' Both men knew immediately that this was a good starting point for a new character and set of sketches. But would this be visual enough for television and the stage show? They knew that they needed more depth to make it work – which was when they decided that their middle-aged husband would order his bride sight unseen over the internet. And that she would look very different in real life to the description on her web page.

'We thought this was the perfect slow-burn sketch,' says David. 'Audiences would get the visual side first, with Ting Tong a lot fatter and older than he had expected. And then we could bring her behaviour into the frame as well, having her flex her muscles gradually and end up taking over her husband's life.'

Having had these early ideas the pair set down to work out an entire back history for the new characters. Even if it is never needed in a sketch, they want their characters' full backgrounds written down to use as reference points for the future. Dates and places of birth, family members, education, friends and experiences to date – it all goes on file so they really know the people they are playing. 'You need a beginning, a middle and an end to a character as well as a sketch,' says David. 'Just copying from life never really works in these kind of shows because you need to define the characters really strongly.'

With that done, the final step, of course, is then to decide who will play the characters in question. The pair say they rarely start out with any fixed casting in mind: 'Sometimes we do both end up wanting to play a certain role,' admits David, though practicalities often dictate that one of them is ultimately more appropriate for the part than the other. Matt's baby face was always going to be best for Ting Tong, while few actors play kindly, put-upon men as well as David, so the latter was obvious for the part of the soon-to-be downtrodden Mr Dudley. From then on, it was down to their long-term hair and make-up designer Lisa Cavalli-Green and her team to create and record the look that would bring the script to life.

'Euphoric. Over the moon. And very, very relieved.' That's how Matt summed up the pair's feelings after that first emotional evening in Portsmouth. Over the next couple of weeks, as the tour moved on through Bournemouth, Southend, Plymouth and Sheffield on its way to Manchester, the audience reaction seemed, if anything, to be strengthening. And still the touts were trying to get a slice of the action. The standard £25 tickets for shows at the country's huge arenas in Cardiff, Birmingham, Glasgow and the like were attracting around three dozen bidders and finally selling for up to £130 each on eBay, where a thriving and lucrative secondary market had sprung up. Outside the theatres the queues for returns were still as long as those for all the *Little Britain* merchandising that had sprung up to accompany the tour.

And the pair certainly didn't get bored while performing. In Brighton, on their eighth week on the road, they were halfway through one of their favourite Daffyd sketches, for example, when Denise Van Outen walked on to the stage with a live camera crew in her wake. 'Ladies and Gentlemen, I am ever so sorry to interrupt your performance,' she said, as Matt froze and the audience tried to work out what was going on. 'As you are probably aware, tonight in London is the British Comedy Awards Live and I am very, very pleased to announce that the winners for Best TV Comedy are Matt Lucas and David Walliams for *Little Britain*.'

As the south-coast audience took to its feet and awards host Jonathan Ross tried to make himself heard through the cheers, Matt and David thanked their television director Declan Lowney, their producer Geoff Posner – and their fans. The impromptu interruption added hugely to the success of the Brighton night and after the encores that evening the BBC cameras came back, this time to Matt's dressing room, where the pair were awarded something they coveted even more: the inaugural Ronnie Barker Writer of the Year Award.

Ronnie Corbett, a long-time fan of *Little Britain*, had introduced the new prize at the London ceremony. The Writers' Guild of Great Britain had decided to rename the long-standing writers' award in memory of Ronnie Barker, the *Two Ronnies* to *Open All Hours* star, who had died earlier in the year. As Ronnie Barker's widow Joy watched from the audience in London, Ronnie Corbett announced that Matt and David would be the first to collect his annual award. And in Brighton they were almost overcome at the news. 'It is simply amazing to get an award with Ronnie Barker's name on it, we don't feel worthy at all,' said David.

'We are huge fans of what *The Two Ronnies* did and what Ronnie Barker did as a writer. It's just a great, great honour,' added Matt.

Leaving the Brighton Centre that night the pair signed more autographs at the stage door than ever – the signings could take almost half an hour at some venues. But neither begrudged the time or the effort. And with two top comedy awards to take back to their hotel, they had more reason than normal to be smiling.

That night, even Matt was happy to be on the road and on tour. As a lifelong Arsenal fan he had said his big regret about doing a national tour in 2005–06 had been missing almost all of the team's final games at Highbury. With an accolade from one of his childhood comedy heroes in his pocket, though, the sacrifice finally felt worth it. And as winter turned to spring the pair were into the groove with the tour. Different audiences and venues created some ever-changing dynamics and kept them permanently on their toes. But the basics of their act were now second nature. They had long since said that 2006 wouldn't give them enough time to write, rehearse and film a fourth series of *Little Britain*. But they were working on a Christmas special for the end of the year. And as they criss-crossed the country they started people-watching again – a habit both had formed as children and one that had brought them together as friends some 15 years earlier.

Between shows in their hotels and at restaurants they started to talk to each other about what they had seen – and they started to laugh about it. Towards the end of 2005, some critics had said the pair would never film another prime-time BBC series. Halfway through the following year, they had both decided that they were going to do just that. When the tour was over, they would go straight back to work. Making people laugh had got them both through difficult childhoods. And they vowed they weren't going to stop doing it now.

CHAPTER 2

A SUBURBAN BOY

'Get Wiggy! Get him!' Half a dozen boys in the playground of a small Hertfordshire school broke off from their football game when one of them spotted a familiar figure trying to edge unseen towards the classrooms. Eleven-year-old Matt Lucas had arrived for school and another day of bullying was set to begin.

By his own admission, Matt was an obvious target for the playground bullies. He was chubby, shy and introverted. While he was a massive football fan, he wasn't a great player, and unlike his pop-loving classmates he was nerdily obsessed by the television stars and comedies of yesteryear. Worst of all, of course, Matt was completely bald.

Born in Paddington, London, on 5 March 1974, Matthew Richard Lucas was brought up in Stanmore, Middlesex. When Matt was young, his dad John ran a chauffeur company and then became a business consultant, while his mother Diana looked after the blond-haired Matt and his elder brother Howard. Looking back, they all agree it was a typically happy, middle-class childhood. They had a close extended family, they attended bar mitzvahs and weddings, played with the neighbours and were almost indistinguishable from millions of similar suburban families across the country.

Or at least they had been until Matt was hit by a car on holiday in Portugal at the age of four. His terrified family rushed him to hospital, prayed that his injuries wouldn't turn out to be life-threatening and held him close when they were told he would make a complete recovery. Back in Britain, everyone tried to put the accident behind them and go on as normal – and that was when Matt's hair first fell out.

Doctors say the reasons behind this sort of event are unclear – though it is common for people to conjecture about them. 'Many people think that accidents or sudden shock can turn someone's hair white or make it fall out overnight, though this is really something of a myth,' says hospital consultant and television doctor Ashley Brown. 'Genetic factors are more likely to be at play and people who do lose their hair suddenly may well grow it back over the course of several months.'

This seems to be what happened to Matt. His hair started to grow back within weeks of the family's return to Britain and over the next few years the accident really was all but forgotten. But then, one morning ,the seven-year-old Matt woke to find great clumps of hair on his pillow once again. Over the next few weeks, every strand of his hair was to fall out a second time – it was *alopecia totalis* and this time the doctors said it would never grow back. To this day, Matt puts a brave face on the event, saying it never bothered him as much as people assume it did. But his frustration is hard to hide altogether. 'That was the trick God played on me – to give me back my hair and then take it away for good,' he says, before changing the subject, looking away and refusing to say any more on the matter.

At the time, however, people had plenty to say, and plenty of suggestions about his hair loss. 'I suffered the gamut of quack homeopathic remedies, pills, acupuncture, seaweed rubbed into my head, everything,' he says. And after endless doctors and hospital appointments, Matt was finally issued with an NHS wig. The idea was to have it in time for his transfer from primary to secondary school, where everyone feared that the older children might not be as kind as the younger ones. With a decent wig, none of these new schoolmates need know that Matt had no hair. He could be treated like everyone else and would fit in or fall on his own merits. The problem, however, was that in the early 1980s the NHS didn't offer specific wigs for children. All that the doctors could offer Matt was one designed for a woman. And, unfortunately, it showed.

Staring endlessly at his reflection in the mirror at home, Matt didn't know if he had the guts to wear it. And, even if he did, he wasn't sure if he wanted to – it itched furiously after about an hour and left him desperate to pull it off. As usual, the entire Lucas family rallied around, however. After a few snips and an attempt at restyling, everyone tried to reassure Matt that it looked OK, while his aunt sewed a cotton handkerchief to the inner mesh to try and make it more comfortable.

After days of confidence-building, Matt finally took a deep breath and wore the wig to his primary school as a sort of dummy run for later in the year. But things didn't go well. 'That very first day a kid ripped the wig off, threw it on to the floor and ran past laughing.' From then on it seemed to become a rite of passage for other kids in the playground to try and knock the wig off their classmate's head as well – despite all the best actions of the teachers and other parents to try and calm the situation. To make matters worse, the 'Wiggy' nickname was added to all the others that he had endured to date. His dream of keeping a low profile at senior school seemed unlikely to come true – and at just 12 years old Matt decided that he had had enough. He was bald, pure and simple, and he vowed to stay that way rather than try to cover it up. The wig was shoved into the bottom of a drawer back at home and he headed back to school without it.

It was a brave move for someone who says all he had ever wanted was to fit in and to be left to make the most of school like every other child. And it needed all the young lad's growing sense of determination to see the decision through, because the low-level bullying and taunting he had suffered so far would continue for many more years. 'I don't like to talk about it, but it was fucking relentless,' he admitted years later.

While Matt is on record as saying that having no hair could be a blessing rather than a curse, it is clear that the mental scars are still to heal fully. He claimed that he had found hair 'incredibly irritating' when he had had it. 'I hated having it cut because I remember it going down the back of my neck and being itchy,' he says. 'I also hated having my hair washed. I had quite long hair, a bit like Andy, from Lou and Andy, and I used to get nits. As a kid all I ever really wanted was a short-back-and-sides.' Bearing in mind how things turned out, it is a salutary warning to be careful about what you wish for.

Back in the security of his family home, Matt's daytime traumas always seemed to fade away. But like millions of other people who are bullied or abused at school, Matt sought refuge in food – and as he entered his teenage years his weight started to balloon. At home, his mother introduced a series of diets and exercise regimes to try and bring her son back to size, but nothing seemed to work. When he reached the age of 13 (and looked like he might soon hit the same weight in stones), she decided to get outside help and took him to their local Weight Watchers group.

Perhaps unsurprisingly, Matt was the only child in a class full of middle-aged women – and he is constantly asked if his experiences there formed the basis of the Fat Fighters sketches with the awful Marjorie 'I am my target weight' Dawes. It is something Matt has always denied,

19

though his mother says there is an uncanny physical resemblance between her and Matt's Marjorie.

And, while Matt refuses to indulge in the tears-of-a-clown cliché of a comedian endlessly reliving a tortured childhood to justify his comedy routines, he does admit that the Weight Watchers classes triggered the start of the people-watching phase that has never left him. At just 13, he somehow felt the need to store up his memories of the weight-loss classes and all the people in them. Time has played some tricks on those early impressions – the mother pushing her reluctant son through the doors and into the room, the class leader who tried to make him feel special, all the other women in the room who struggled with their own self-esteem and tried desperately to help him with his. He didn't know why, but he knew that one way or another he would remember them all.

Back at school, Matt was also starting to feel some peer pressure to succeed. He had won a scholarship to the results-oriented Haberdashers' Aske's school in Borehamwood, whose previous old boys included Alan Wicker and arts journalist and commentator Brian Sewell. And while the school had been founded on money left by a City of London silk merchant in 1689 it seemed to have comedy on its curriculum in the mid-1980s. David Baddiel was one of Matt's near contemporaries, for example, alongside Ali G creator Sacha Baron Cohen.

Sacha, as a teenager, was already displaying some unexpected talents. 'When I think back to Sacha, I mostly just remember him break-dancing on the lino in our kitchen... he was a good friend of my brother Howard,' says Matt. Amazing to think that a dozen or so years later David, Sacha and Matt would all be seen as saviours of British comedy – and that, having once competed in school sports and music days as teenagers, they would now be competing head to head for some of the most prestigious awards in the television industry as adults.

Today, Matt says he feels he owes a lot of his comic imagination and timing to the skills he was forced to learn as a schoolboy in Borehamwood – because he realised at 14 that the best way to win friends and win over the bullies was to do impressions, play the fool and make people laugh. Becoming the class joker certainly seemed to work. He became more popular and was gradually able to relax. Going to school was no longer something he dreaded – Sunday nights were no longer the worst night of his week. But, just as he found ways to accept his appearance and integrate with his peers, a new crisis was about to shoot his equilibrium to pieces. Another part of his comfortable childhood was about to unravel.

After coming home from school one day, he was told that his dad, John, had been arrested for fraud. The family was in turmoil – and the suburban neighbours' net curtains started to twitch. Looking back, Matt's mum Diana says he seemed to be affected more than anyone by the crisis, which gathered momentum as John was sent for trial, found guilty and eventually jailed for four years. 'Matt was very close to his father and it was a very difficult time for him when John was in prison. He found it very hard to deal with, very hard to cope,' she says. What Matt also did was to bottle up his thoughts and fears, speaking very little about what he felt and trying to pretend that everything was OK when it was clear to everyone that it wasn't.

Former neighbours said the local community's reaction made matters worse – with plenty of gossip and finger-pointing meaning Matt and Howard were shunned by several of their local friends. Neither of them knew the names of all the self-appointed moral guardians who began to look down on the Lucas family when John went to prison. But Matt in particular would never forget how they acted. Once again, he stored the impressions away for the future, never knowing when they might be useful or when these characters might one day see the light of day again.

Over the next couple of years, Matt and Howard got used to the routine of prison visits and in many ways they drew closer to their father through letters and phone calls. But Diana was feeling the strain of being alone – and when John came home after nearly four years inside she told him their marriage was over. She filed for divorce and John spent very little time back in his old house with his two teenage boys. Once again the more sensitive Matt took the break-up hard, desperately upset that his fractured home life was not getting the instant repair he had been hoping for.

'Trust me, I have the classic psychological make-up of

a comedian,' he told *Times* reporter Simon Fanshawe years later, when his angry and expletive-filled stand-up comedy was first starting to get him noticed. 'I know what it is like to have people close to me dying, go to prison, get divorced and have accidents. I know life can be hard.'

He also knew that tough times can leave their mark for years. 'Do I get depressed? Of course I do, I'm a comedian,' he added when asked about how his childhood moulded him. But for all that he has always said that he didn't spend all his schooldays in total isolation. The fledgling friendships he had been making as class clown just before his dad got arrested did hold firm through the ensuing trauma. Other talents also got him noticed. He was the drummer in a school band (and in *Shooting Stars* his drum kit would get a far larger audience than it had ever done in Middlesex, though the clothes Matt wore to play it all those years later would be a little different). Matt also had several childhood brushes with fame. He wrote to *Jim'll Fix It* asking to sit on the bean bag at the start of the show – and got his wish. One morning, he got to ask a celebrity question on *Saturday Superstore* and he also auditioned and won a role in the kids chorus of a West End musical, though this never saw the light of day.

For a time, he also got to be a part of his school's in-crowd. 'There was a group who were young and beautiful and took drugs and had sex with each other. It was very exciting,' he remembers. Matt, though, didn't always do himself any favours in the battle to fit in. 'I remember one Saturday-night party turning off the stereo and putting on a video of *Modern Times*, the Charlie Chaplin film, and saying, "Look at this, guys, it's genius!" But I didn't get quite the reaction I had been hoping for. They were all smoking dope and shagging on the bed with the coats on it and I was extremely unpopular for trying to persuade them to stop and watch my favourite film. I suppose I got away with it by being the eccentric of the group.'

For all his eccentricities, Matt says he was comfortable with the cool kids – as they seemed to be with him. 'These were people I could genuinely describe as friends. We had much in common, including our sense of humour. It's just that they would put on a bootleg *Clockwork Orange* video and I would put on *Modern Times*.'

He was still lousy at playing football, but Matt had fallen in love with watching the game – of which a lot more later. And while an Arsenal season ticket was one of the first things he bought when he started earning real money in his late twenties, one of his most treasured possessions as a teenager was a photograph of him standing next to legendary goalkeeper Peter Shilton. Shilton's not an Arsenal player, but you can't have everything, Matt would say when he showed off the snap to his friends. And strictly speaking the photograph wasn't exactly genuine either – Matt was grinning inanely next to Shilton's waxwork at Madame Tussaud's rather than standing with the man himself. But for a teenage football fan with stars in his eyes it still felt like a pretty cool possession to have.

Back at school, Matt also found release and refuge on stage – not least because dressing up for a role meant the teenager could often wear a wig or a hat and forget about his baldness for a while. And while he did apparently shine as Mr Hardcastle in Oliver Goldsmith's *She Stoops to Conquer*, in an early sign of things to come many of the other roles Matt was offered back then were of women. Interestingly enough, most of them were also in comedies.

As his late teens approached, Matt was, finally, on an even keel. School life hadn't been easy, he missed his dad and his personal life had brought more than its fair share of challenges. But he had made it through them all and was far from bitter about the past. Did all of the bad times affect your childhood? he was once asked as an adult. 'No,' he said. 'But because of them I did watch more television than was normal.'

It was a simple and typically self-deprecating observation on the way he dealt with everything life had thrown at him. And while he didn't know it at the time, another troubled schoolboy was living his life in a similar manner. Some 35 miles across London in leafy, suburban Surrey, this other teenager was also hiding away in his bedroom and watching an equally excessive amount of television. His name was David Williams.

CHAPTER 3

ANOTHER SUBURBAN BOY

There is a school of thought that people brought up in Britain's suburbs have one of two distinct mindsets. One group look out of their windows as children and dream of falling in love, starting a family and living the same happy life as their parents. The other group look out of the same windows and dream only of escape. David Walliams, whose surname back then was the more conventional 'Williams', says he was slap bang in the middle of the latter category.

'Banstead is a sleepy suburban place where nothing happens. As I grew up I was screaming for glamour, for excitement, for danger. For all the things you didn't get in Surrey,' he says – though he admits he spent most of his childhood fantasising about all sorts of bizarre horrors that might be going on behind the town's neatly cut front lawns. His imagination had pretty much plotted out a British version of *Desperate Housewives* long before the American show ever hit the screens. And like Matt, many of David's childhood fantasies would one day be revived in the most popular *Little Britain* sketches.

Born on 20 August 1971, David had an elder sister Julie, who now works as a primary school teacher. His dad Peter earned a decent income as an engineer with London Transport while his mum Kathleen was a lab technician in a local school.

'To posh people we're not posh, but we went on holiday abroad and had a Vauxhall Cavalier and I definitely had a life of privilege,' he says when asked about his childhood. 'I led a sheltered life. I never encountered poverty and I did all the usual things, such as swimming and Cubs.' And he took a long time to find his comedy voice. 'My sister Julie always used to entertain guests with her Pam Ayres poems. She delighted people. I always appalled them,' he claims. 'Julie and I always vied for attention, but she was the comedienne. I certainly don't remember my parents or anyone else finding me funny in any way.'

Like most children, David was always trying to assume new identities to try and shake off the boredom he felt at home. He put a sign saying 'David Williams: Private Detective' on his bedroom door as a homage to his childhood hero Sherlock Holmes. And he constantly tried to drag Julie off on adventures where they could look for clues, find hidden treasures and solve Scooby Doo-style crimes.

Written down on paper, it seems like a very ordinary, provincial childhood. But David's behaviour wasn't entirely normal – and, while his parents did try to humour him, they were starting to worry about where it might lead. Dressing up was the biggest issue, as was play-acting like a girl. 'When I was as young as three or something, my sister used to dress me up in bridesmaid's dresses and stuff from her dressing-up box. I loved it – I encouraged it,' he says. And as time passed he needed even less encouragement to pull on women's clothing. One summer, when visiting his sister's guide camp, the blond-haired David unaccountably found, put on and posed for photographs in a bikini belonging to one of the other mothers.

Back at home, one of the young David's other favourite party tricks was to sweep downstairs in the mornings in a rich silk dressing gown, swirl it around him and ask to be called – for reasons no one can remember – Davina. His parents felt he needed to toughen up; they were worried that he would be bullied at school if his tastes didn't change. So they were over the moon when he jumped at the chance to join the rough and tumble of the Navy Cadets – relief that was tempered years later when their son admitted that he had only ever signed up because he wanted to dress up in a sailor suit every Wednesday afternoon.

So would this sensitive child cope in the very masculine world of the fee-paying Reigate Grammar School? One of the top independent schools in Britain, it had been a boys-only establishment until 1976, less than six years before David arrived. And it didn't become fully co-educational until long after he had left – so everyone was worried that the boy who jokingly liked to be called Davina was in for a tough few years. For a while, everyone appeared to have been right.

'I don't know why, but I was very camp from a very early age, so of course I was bullied,' he says of his first experiences at secondary school.

At home, his parents were desperately worried about how their son would cope and whether he might get physically as well as mentally hurt by his classmates. But, as it turned out, David was somehow one step ahead of the game. Like Matt, who had turned into the class clown to take attention away from his baldness, David played the fool to stop people getting too hung up on his play-acting. Both were learning valuable comic lessons from a very early age.

For David, this meant throwing aside the persona of Davina that he had formulated at home – and taking on a new role as Daphne in school. 'For some reason the boys used to call me Daphne, which I know was meant to put me down. They were punishing me for being different, but my reaction was to embrace it. I turned it around quite nicely, actually. Then after a while they all started looking at me to entertain them. It was a great way to defuse things and they would actually shout for me: "Daphne! Daphne!" The taunts never made me cry, because I am terribly attention-seeking and I was the kind of person who got bullied and loved the attention of it.'

So, as it turned out, David's parents' worst fears were

never realised. Far from being ostracised or beaten up at school, their son ended up finding a decent network of close friends. And it seemed that dressing up in women's clothing might actually do wonders for both his academic and love life. 'Dressing up as a woman was always the first idea I had about anything. I remember we had to make a video in business studies and this girl I really fancied, called Amy, put make-up on me. I found it incredibly exciting. And when I was at university I went out with this actress called Katy and she liked dressing me up as well.' A pattern, as they say, had begun to emerge.

In fact, even before meeting Amy and Katy, David had already fallen in love: with drama. The teachers at Reigate Grammar worked hard to make time for several stage performances a term, including dramas, comedies and musicals. David loved them all and soon realised that if he volunteered for some of the female roles that no one else wanted to play he was likely to be cast in almost everything. And, unlike the unwilling contemporaries who were forced to drag up for a performance, David's past experience at dressing up made him a natural. Former schoolmates say he was always ready to go the extra mile and wear wigs, make-up and dresses to ensure his female characters were as convincing as possible – as several cast photographs prove.

What David didn't do was get into his school's sporting heritage. Team sports left him cold – both as a player and as a fan. So, while his schoolmates were watching *Grandstand*, he was catching up on old-fashioned comedies, which had begun to be something of an obsession with him. He was also a voracious viewer of newer comedy and variety shows – and got an early taste for replicating and spoofing them.

'The highlights of my year were always the two class assemblies, where I was able to put on spoofs of TV shows like *Game for a Laugh* and get teachers to come up and put custard pies and flour bombs in their faces. That was my refuge and I would be the hero of the school until break time.'

Whether he was aware of it or not, what David was also doing in these spoofs and skits was practising his craft. And he showed an early willingness to learn from the experts. In the late 1980s, Dame Edna Everage was one of the biggest names in British entertainment and a near permanent fixture on television. Perhaps unsurprisingly, David was a huge fan of her alter ego Barry Humphries – and he was determined to find out more about him. At home, he watched tapes of Humphries's shows time and time again, trying to work out which gestures and moves made the audience laugh, trying to decide which lines were scripted, which were ad-libbed and whether any of that even mattered. One thing he knew for certain was that Dame Edna was a character in her prime, in total control of her act. So when a new Everage London show was announced, the 17-year-old David knew he had to see it live. He got the train into town, headed to the Theatre Royal, Drury Lane, and bought the best seat he could afford. Every penny, he says, was well spent. 'It was an absolutely inspirational moment to see the show,' he says. And so he went back to see it again, just in case there was anything he had missed.

Years later, when *Little Britain* was winning just about every industry award available, David said he got the biggest buzz when the comedy heroes he had followed since childhood said that they loved his work. Ronnie Corbett's praise was particularly cherished – but for a long time Barry Humphries's affirmation meant the most. When the Australian told David that *Little Britain* was pure comedy gold, it was like going full circle back to those teenage years in Surrey. It felt like all the bad years, and all the struggles, had been worthwhile.

Back in Banstead, there were still some problems to sort out, though. Just like Matt, David's weight had soared in his teenage years – by 16, he reckons he was the second chubbiest in his school and could have been the real inspiration behind the Fat Fighters sketches with Marjorie Dawes. He also had some unlikely goals to tell his career advisers – apart from Barry Humphries, his biggest role model was the actor Michael Gambon. But no one at Reigate Grammar School really thought the awkward teenager who always played women in school plays could ever one day emulate the gritty National Theatre star.

What David didn't have, back then, was an ordinary social life. 'I think my parents were dying for me to go out and get drunk and act like a normal teenager,' he says.

'Instead, I would spend Saturday nights with my friend Robin watching *Brideshead Revisited* on video. We used to take walks around Hampton Court Gardens, quoting Evelyn Waugh.'

And it was on one of those walks that David spotted something that would help change his life. It happened one sunny spring day, when he and Robin saw a tall and elegant lady walking towards them from around the corner of the palace. She was wearing immaculate, if old-fashioned clothes, and from a distance she looked utterly perfect, so measured, so mannered, so genteel. But, while Robin carried on chatting, oblivious to anything out of the ordinary, the teenage David found himself puzzled. He was sure that something about the picture ahead of him wasn't quite right, but he had no idea why that was. Was this lady a famous actress, or did he recognise her from school or from one of the shops in Reigate? Had they perhaps stumbled on to a film set, and were they on camera? But there were no signs that anything about that corner of the park was in any way unusual.

David walked on, frowning just slightly and hardly concentrating on his friend's story. And then it hit him. From around six feet away, he realised that this perfect, genteel lady wasn't, in fact, a lady after all. She was a man. It wasn't the height, he said later, that gave it away. Instead, it seemed to be something else, perhaps a heaviness that had nothing to do with weight, an overemphasis on every movement, the kind you often get when you are drunk and are trying not to show it.

As they approached each other on the gravel path, David was desperate not to show that he was staring – or that he had rumbled the so-called lady's game. He suddenly felt an overwhelming sense of empathy and respect for this strange man's bravery. For the sheer courage he must have, in order to put on those clothes and believe that he could fit in and pass unnoticed in a harsh and intrusive world. For the willingness the man must feel to suffer abuse or humiliation just because he wanted to be different.

As they did finally pass each other and head their separate ways, David forced himself not to turn around. And, anyway, he hardly needed to. Over the past few minutes he had somehow burned every detail of the figure into his memory. One day he would remember him, he decided.

Back at home, supposedly preparing for his A levels, David started to turn his life around. He had a Saturday job as a lifeguard at a local swimming pool and between shifts he started entertaining his colleagues with Rowan Atkinson sketches. The reaction was so good that other people asked to see his mini-performances and to everyone's surprise David's circle of friends finally started to grow. He also decided he would have to lose some weight if he ever wanted to look good in clothes and get a girlfriend, both of which he soon achieved.

And while Michael Gambon remained his theatrical idol, David's key obsession continued to be television comedy. He would watch hour after hour of shows and learned dozens of sketches off by heart. And in the process he noticed something. Yes, Barry Humphries was a fantastic solo performer, as were the likes of Dick Emery and Kenny Everett. But the majority of big names in comedy didn't seem to work alone. Eric Morecambe, Ernie Wise, Ronnie Corbett and Ronnie Barker weren't exactly cutting-edge cool among the teenagers of Banstead in the 1980s, but David recognised the class behind their performances. He could even find humour in the likes of Little and Large and Cannon and Ball. And he would be one of the first to really spot the new wave of comedy double acts when the likes of Vic Reeves and Bob Mortimer started getting mentioned in the papers and making their first appearances on late-night review programmes. If he wanted to emulate these guys, David knew he too would need a collaborator. He needed a co-conspirator to plan and perform with – and so far no one he could think of from school, the swimming pool or anywhere else seemed to fit the bill. With his A levels out of the way, David decided to look further afield.

CHAPTER 4

LEARNING THE ROPES

Making it big in comedy can be all about contacts. And Matt, for one, started to make some good ones very early. He was still at Haberdashers' Aske's school when he auditioned along with some 2,500 other 10- to 19-year-olds to take classes at the National Youth Music Theatre – and once selected he started to realise just how many other talented performers he would be competing against if he was ever going to make it as a professional.

'Jude Law and Jonny Lee Miller were there at the same time as me and even though they were only about 14 they were absolutely brilliant. I could have told you then that they would become big stars,' he says, having sat open mouthed in the audience one evening watching Jude as Adrenaline and Jonny as Virus in a Richard Stilgoe musical called *Bodywork*.

'Our best young performers are fearless,' confirmed Jeremy James Taylor, who had been the artistic director of the NYMT for 25 years by the time Matt took up his place.

Famous in the industry as one of the shrewdest talent-spotters in the business, Jeremy says some of his students have 'a sort of Ready Brek glow around them' even at the auditions stage. And a year after trying to learn from Jude and Jonny, Matt was trying to acquire this glow himself as he auditioned against more than 4,000 other youngsters for a place at the equally prestigious National Youth Theatre.

Founded in 1956, the NYT teaches everything from acting and stage management to costume design and lighting. And it has a reputation as the place where stars are born. Establishment names such as Ben Kingsley, Derek Jacobi and Helen Mirren all trained there, while more recent graduates include Daniel Day-Lewis, Liza Tarbuck, Orlando Bloom, Jamie Theakston and Daniel Craig. It operates in summer schools and holiday courses across the country and its students put on a regular series of productions and tours – all of which must be of professional standard. The hours are long and students at the London centre are encouraged to use their spare time to see as many other plays or productions as possible. Graduates say it is a form of immersion therapy into the performing arts and that you either love it or hate it.

Matt, of course, loved it from the start. He loved the work, he loved the performing, he loved the people. As far as his confidence and his personal life were concerned, he also loved the feeling that his appearance no longer caused much of a stir. In such a competitive world, he realised, it could even do him some favours and get him noticed.

While Matt settled down to his first full-on experience of the NYT, the slightly older David was thriving on his second season. He too loved the work and the performing. But his biggest love was of the people he met there. After so many years of feeling he was drowning in the sleepy Surrey suburbs, he was over the moon to be in London among such a diverse crowd of students. For, despite having more than its fair share of theatrical, middle-class children in its ranks, the NYT does make huge efforts to include people from all backgrounds and from all over the country. The mini melting-pot atmosphere was something David had only ever dreamed of before. They weren't quite the 'kids from *Fame*', but they were the closest thing to it that he had ever encountered, and it felt fantastic.

'Hey, Dave, there's a boy over there who does a brilliant Jimmy Savile impression. You have to hear it. He looks a bit weird but he's hilarious.' It was 1990 and a big group of the NYT summer-school students were lounging around taking a break in a theatre bar in north London. David looked up. He had found a good group of friends and for the first time in his life he felt like the leader of the pack. His own party trick was to do what everyone said was a brilliant impression of Frankie Howerd. So the last thing he felt he wanted was a younger rival who could make more laughs by playing someone else. 'My friends said I should meet this other guy but I was actually a bit piqued about the whole thing,' he says. 'I thought, He's a rival, I don't want to meet him, I want to be known as the funny one who does all the funny impressions. But I went over, we got introduced, I did my impression and he did his, and we were like, "OK. Let's go back to our respective groups now and entertain them," which we did.'

The competitive crisis averted, the pair kept their distance for the rest of the summer school. But both were secretly impressed at the other's ability and wondered if they would ever meet again.

Exactly one year later, they did. That year's class was putting on *The Tempest* as its end-of-term play, and David (playing to his strengths) had been cast as Trinculo, the drunken court jester. 'There were some hugely talented young actors in the group that year, but I was more than happy with a comic part,' he says.

Matt, meanwhile, was working behind the scenes helping move the sets. And, while Trinculo was hardly one of the leading roles in the production, Matt was convinced that the man who had done the Frankie Howerd impression a year earlier still had the fabled 'Ready Brek glow'. It was just like being back at the NYMT with Jude Law and Jonny Lee Miller on stage, he said. 'When we first did the impressions for each other, I immediately thought David was absolutely hilarious,' Matt says. 'I then saw he was a really talented actor as well.'

Despite being nearly three years David's junior, Matt plucked up the courage to say hello one afternoon while the actor was waiting in the wings for his cues. After the day's rehearsals had finished, they started to talk properly – and have hardly stopped since.

The conversations started with a quick run-through of as many impressions as they could think of – which took quite some time. And, while they conjured up the voices of so many past and present comedians, they realised they shared an incredibly similar, and very specific, sense of humour. For a start, both were near obsessive fans of the sprawling, surreal and slapstick comedy in *Vic Reeves Big Night Out*, the first mainstream television show staring Vic and his comedy partner Bob Mortimer.

Matt and David started acting out some of those sketches – and imagining other ones. What really excited them both was the fact that they shared the same nerdy comedy heritage. How many people of their age were obsessively into Laurel and Hardy, for example? Matt and David were. How many had ever heard of characters such as Arthur Lucan's music-hall creation Old Mother Riley? Matt and David had – and they could repeat all her best lines. They were also ready with impressions of Mona Lott and all the other characters from the catchphrase-laden wartime comedy *It's That Man Again*, aka *ITMA*. 'It's being so cheerful as keeps me going,' the boys would repeat, as Mona had done in almost every episode.

Throw in an encyclopaedic knowledge of variety acts such as Wilson, Kepple and Betty from the 1930s and 1940s and it was obvious that Matt and David couldn't be better suited. Both put Charlie Chaplin on a pedestal, and listed his black-and-white 1940 film *The Great Dictator* as one of their all-time favourites. Interestingly enough, echoes from this film would be heard years later in the boys' own work. Chaplin directed the comedy, as well as playing dual central roles as a Jewish barber and a dictator whose initials are AH — pretty easy to guess who was being hinted at in the 1940s. There was a clever mix of both over-the-top slapstick and subtle satire in the plot, a feeling that grew right from the opening titles, over which a voice boomed out: 'This is the story of the period between two world wars — an interim during which insecurity cut loose, liberty took a nose dive, and humanity was kicked around somewhat.' Close your eyes and you can almost hear Tom Baker saying the lines more than half a century later.

In 1990, Matt and David weren't living entirely in the past, however. Both were equally obsessed with the most up-to-date comedy of the day — and both were already trying to think of ways to get into the business.

'One gloriously sunny Saturday evening when we should have been out having fun, we went down to the video shop, got out the worst film we could find in there, which was *UFO* — which stands for "You Fuck Off" — starring Roy "Chubby" Brown,' remembers David. 'Everyone else we knew would have hated it but we loved it and I loved those times, when it was just fun and you didn't know where it was leading. We would just sit around, dreaming up TV shows for hours on end.' And back then it was just dreaming. 'We certainly weren't thinking, Oh, we're going to make some money out of this,' David says.

They didn't have a career path, just yet. And, even if

they had worked one out, the end of summer school was going to put everything on hold.

As well-educated boys from upwardly mobile, middle-class families, both Matt and David knew that leaving school and getting a job in the theatre or a television studio was hardly an option for them. That sort of low-paid uncertainty wasn't what their parents had had in mind when they had pushed them towards good schools and emphasised the importance of exams and qualifications. So while they were in different years at school, university was the obvious next step for them both. But which to choose?

If you wanted to be an actor or a comedian in the 1990s, then Cambridge certainly looked the safest bet – as long as you could join the Footlights crowd. A generation earlier, that theatre group, formed in 1883, had given the world the likes of John Cleese, Eric Idle, Peter Cook and Graham Chapman – all good stuff, as far as Matt and David were concerned. But the more recent round of Footlights names didn't inspire as much confidence. There was already something clubby and stuffy about the likes of Emma Thompson, Stephen Fry, Hugh Laurie and even Griff Rhys Jones. So David, who as the elder of the pair was going through the university application process first, did what a growing number of more alternative performers were doing in the 1990s. He went west.

The city of Bristol had been making headlines in the music world for some time – Portishead, Massive Attack,

Tricky and Roni Size had all recently sprung from its streets or were being formed in its bedrooms. And the local university was well on its way to injecting the same kind of edgy dynamism into the world of television. 'Want to be a star? You'll need youth, talent and a drama degree from Bristol University,' was how *Times* journalist Imogen Edwards-Jones described it, as a network of Bristol graduates started to spread its way through the light-entertainment industry.

By the time David filled in his application form, the drama course, the oldest faculty of its kind in Britain, had become one of the most sought-after spots on the higher-education map. Only around 50 places were available on the course each year – and far more than 50 potential students applied for each of them. In the late 1980s and early 1990s, even getting invited in for an interview meant you had beaten a huge number of your student rivals. But it certainly didn't mean that the challenge was over.

At just 17, a nervous but excited David did his best to shine in the hour-long creative workshop that kicked off the assessment programme. Next up was a group seminar with around half a dozen other hopeful teenagers and mature students. Then there was an individual interview with drama department heads where, among other things, you had to discuss the written submissions you had already sent in about why you wanted to get on to the course. It was tough stuff – but two months after the ordeal had ended David was over the moon to get a letter offering him a place. Having got the necessary A-level grades, he turned up for his first day of term and never looked back.

David was in the Department of Drama, Theatre, Film & Television, to give it its full name. And he loved each of the four elements of its brief. A lot of the work was theoretical rather than practical, but as an avid reader David was more than happy to pore over play texts and explore the social history that had surrounded the writing of them. Students had access to a fully functioning on-site theatre, a cinema and video-viewing complex and, most excitingly of all for David, a set of broadcast-standard film- and video-making equipment. For the first time in his life he felt close to the magical world of television he had loved since childhood. But he was no longer just watching it from a suburban bedroom. He was on his way to finding out how to get inside the box itself.

What David also found from the very start of the three-year degree course was that he was in very good company – his fellow students were as dedicated as he was and the sensitive Surrey schoolboy started to blossom in his new dramatic pastures. And, just as Matt had done a few years earlier at the National Youth Music Theatre, David started to make some pretty impressive contacts.

Matthew Warchus, who among many other things would move into films and direct the West End hit *Art*, was a few years above David. But when David arrived Matthew still cast a large shadow over the department, as did the controversial playwright Mark Ravenhill whose works such as *Shopping and F***king* had made him the scourge of Middle England. These were people David had dreamed of spending time with and from whom he was determined to learn. And they were only the tip of the Bristol iceberg. His other contemporaries, many of whom would still be there when Matt subsequently signed up for the same course, included a lucky half-dozen who would work together for years to come.

There was Jon Rowlands, the Sports Relief producer who also worked with Alexei Sayle and Lenny Beige actor Steve Furst. Simon Pegg, who would end up dominating ITV's *Faith in the Future* as well as *24 Hour Party People*, *Spaced* and *Shaun of the Dead*, was a close friend. As was Dominic Diamond, who would share screen time with David for years before carving out his own niche as a games guru – and also appearing in *Spaced*. David Young, who worked as a producer immediately after leaving Bristol and then became Head of Light Entertainment at the BBC, was another powerhouse fellow student. Then, of course, there was Marcus Brigstocke, who became BBC New Comedian of the Year in 1996 and has hardly stopped working since. The final member of the six-some would turn out to be the most important to Matt and David, however. She was Myfanwy Moore – and her name would ultimately be in the production credits of almost every show they have ever made.

However, at the time, the group denied they had any

plans to take over the airwaves after graduating from Bristol. 'It is a very informal mafia. This is not some south-west version of *Peter's Friends* where people meet up and try and work out where to dominate next year,' said Jon Rowlands.

'It's certainly not a nepotism thing and we haven't stayed together in the Cambridge Footlights fashion. But we do get to work together because we are aware of what each other can do,' added Simon Pegg.

And over the three-year course this meant just about everything. 'It was all about painting yourself purple or running around naked on stage,' remembers Diamond. And it was also all about the hard work that goes into producing top-notch performances.

'We spent a huge amount of time scrutinising popular culture, which gave us all very high standards, particularly with our own work,' says Moore. 'We all became very disciplined writers and our own severest critics. And I think the course helped us to get all the pretension out of our system. When I started, I wanted to work on documentaries and be the world's biggest feminist. I came out wanting to work on the *Late Show* and then got into comedy.'

Matt and David certainly thrived in the hot-house atmosphere of the university's drama department. Having never really been in the in-crowd at school, David in particular loved the small-world feel he got in Bristol, where you really could be a big fish in a small, if extraordinarily talented, pond. This feeling was intensified by the fact that the drama students found they were somehow distanced from the rest of the student body – which seemed to suit just about everybody. 'We seemed to exist in a sort of happy-clappy environment where we didn't mix with anyone else,' said Brigstocke. 'Drama is not like a "9–5 study and then get pissed" course. It's a "midday to 10pm" kind of thing that involves a lot of personal energy. Consequently, people get to know each other very well indeed.'

And, while the course itself was primarily theoretical, everyone spent a lot of time working on the practical side when the lectures and seminars were over. Some past drama students had helped set up what had begun as an amateur comedy night at the Dome Bar in the student-filled Clifton neighbourhood. The weekly event – called 'David Ike and The Orphans of Jesus' – had a rowdy reputation. But it was a perfect place for the students to cut their comedy teeth and face up to their first group of hecklers. David in particular was keen to get on stage there as soon as possible – teaming up with a range of partners along the way. One of the first of his collaborators was Myfanwy Moore, and while they were a hit some nights they got some pretty bad reactions on others. 'We were writing new material and performing it every week, which was brilliant practice. But we were still booed off stage many times when it didn't quite work out,' she recalls.

For his part, David almost got thrown even further off track after seeing Rowan Atkinson in the street one day on a trip to London. 'He was my comedy hero and I asked for his autograph and asked if he had any advice about getting into comedy as a career. "Yes," he said. "Don't." Which sort of took the wind out of my sails for a while.'

Matt was also in London at the time. Nearly three years younger than David, he too had thought long and hard about which university he should attend – or even if he should get a degree at all. His mother had told him that former schoolmates Sacha Baron Cohen and David Baddiel had taken the Cambridge route and were giving the now rather staid world of Footlights a bit of a shake-up. But Matt still wasn't convinced that he wanted to follow them. Having read through prospectus after prospectus and examined everything from drama to journalism courses, he too decided to try for a place at Bristol. But beforehand he decided to do some stand-up of his own.

At 15 he had started to entertain his small circle of friends with the persona of an embittered failed actor with a rich, brandy-soaked voice. It was a character that had been born of watching too many luvvies on self-important arts programmes. He called him Sir Bernard Chumley and three years later Matt wondered if he could work as a comedy character in his own right. He pulled on an endless number of clothes at home trying to get Sir Bernard's look right (and would ultimately top it off with the blond NHS wig he had been given as a child and had left in the bottom of a drawer ever since). In the privacy of his own home, Matt finally felt he had something. But was he really ready to test it out in public?

'You need an amazing confidence to think you are funny enough to do stand-up. You need to believe in yourself and that normally comes with money and class,' says playwright and fellow Bristol graduate Mark Ravenhill. Matt, unfortunately, had neither.

What he had instead, he realised, was a growing sense of anger at the world, a simmering sense of injustice. A desire to take control and get his own back on people and situations that had caused him so much pain in his childhood. He first took to the stage on 3 October 1992 in a tiny comedy club in London called the VD Clinic where new acts were welcome and no one got paid (the joke in the club's name was supposed to be that it stood for Val Doonican rather than venereal disease). Matt had spent many evenings there in the audience seeing how hostile the punters could be. So he decided that offence would be his best form of defence – and that the nice boy from north London was going to leap out of his shell and be as offensive as possible.

'I was a precocious teenager and I was extremely blue,' he remembers. 'I effed and blinded relentlessly and I was notorious for unapologetically bludgeoning my audiences into weary appreciation. Where there was a rude word, I used it. Where there wasn't, I invented it. In fact, I became known amongst my peers as "the cunt comedian" – although in retrospect I am forced to concede that this may not have had anything to do with the language I used. I was rubbish, of course, in all my first performances. At one club I walked on to the stage, said, "Good evening," and the entire audience got up and went to the bar.'

But still something pushed him forward, making him sign up for ever more try-out and open-mike nights. Looking back, he says it was a period when the twin demons in his psyche were battling for dominance. On the one hand, there was an extreme shyness, a desire to build walls around himself and stay apart from a world that he knew could hurt anyone who dared to be different. There was also his very British desire not to make a fuss or be the centre of attention.

When asked once what trait he most deplored in himself, he replied, 'I am prone to bouts of extreme shyness in public, which lead me to lurk in the back of supermarkets with a heavy shopping basket until the shop empties.' It was clearly a joke, a throwaway line. But, while he may never have actually done this in real life, the fact is that he must have thought of it, just to have come up with the answer in the first place. Staying in the shadows, not getting in anyone's way, putting himself last – it is all ingrained into Matt's extraordinarily complex DNA.

Or at least it was until his other demon came to the fore – the one that persuaded him to get on to those stages even as a teenager, to dress up in ridiculous clothes and to risk humiliation on a nightly basis in clubs where he was barely old enough to buy a drink. As a live performer it was the ultimate trial by fire. And for a long time it felt as if Matt was going to fail at it. The reason was simple – he had taken the hardest possible route for someone who wanted to please an audience. He had decided that, instead of trying to win people over and be everyone's funny best friend, he was going to be their worst nightmare. It didn't always work – but he says to this day that he had no alternative.

'I was so young then, just 18, and I looked so strange without any hair and so I felt a certain estrangement from everyone else all the time. I could have tried to go up on the stage and done the old "isn't it always the way?" type of real-life comedy routine, but I didn't feel that I shared that much with the audience, so I didn't think I could pull it off. Instead, I wanted to celebrate difference rather than what we had in common. People didn't understand back then that Sir Bernard was a true representation of me. It was far truer than if I had gone up on stage with a pint in my hand and said, "All right, lads, my name's Matt." That would have been fake. I didn't want to talk about myself, I wanted to escape from myself. That's why I went on stage as a character, and that's why the character I picked was to some degree a monster.'

Funnily enough, there is a huge comedy heritage that backs up Matt's theory. The late Ronnie Barker had once hinted at pretty much the same motivation: 'I feel I have no personality of my own – so I pull on a bizarre character instead and start performing and that's what gets me through it,' he said when asked about his reasons for going on stage. So, despite all the incredulous, often unpleasant audiences, Sir Bernard Chumley was going to stick around. And for a while Matt found he was just a little bit obsessed with him. 'I was still full of angst and I channelled it all into comedy. I was completely focused on it, like a young footballer. When I got going I had no life outside stand-up; I completely buried my head in the sand as far as any social life was concerned.'

So going off to Bristol was the best thing that could have happened to the still shy teenager. And though he initially found it hard to settle down in the intense student environment, he says that his infamously angry alter ego brought him some unexpected benefits. 'I would have had real problems at university if I hadn't done stand-up,' he says in a rare discussion of his feelings. 'It was a release for me and because of it I became a much quieter person, more relaxed and happier. I suddenly felt I was very happy to be in my group of friends and not be the one cracking jokes. I did need to prove it still, but I felt I proved it with my show.'

What he also felt, though, was an undercurrent of snobbery. By working professionally (albeit for free most nights), he thought he had already paid some dues to the entertainment business. And he was convinced that he was far more realistic than many of his student friends about what the public wanted to see. 'When I was training to be an actor, shouting at people wasn't considered to be art,' he said when he looked back on his academic career. 'On my drama course, if you walk into a room and throw meat around you are considered a genius, some kind of theatrical wizard. But if you go on telly you are considered a cunt.' Matt, more than anything, wanted to be on telly and he was entirely focused on turning his dream into reality.

As a means to that end, he was always ready to do any extra work that involved the department's television cameras, studio or editing suite. And one assignment would turn out to be the slow-burn trigger for one of the most famous characters he would ever create. It happened when he and a friend headed out on to the streets of Bristol to put together a short film entitled *How Are You?*. As part of it, Matt stopped passers-by, asked them the central question and recorded their responses. Some were not exactly what anyone had expected – one man said that he was dying, for example, which certainly added to the drama of the piece.

But the real stars were the two young lads hanging around outside the main shopping centre. 'How are you? Are you OK?' Matt asked the younger of the pair, to kick-start the interview. It felt as if it took an age to get a response. The youngster seemed unable to focus his thoughts and answer this simplest of questions. Instead, he simply stood there looking like a rabbit caught in car headlights as the camera rolled. Matt was just about to give up and stop the filming when it happened. The boy started to speak. And he didn't stop. 'Yeah, but, well, I dunno, 'cos, like, yeah…' he began, in an incoherent West Country drawl. Editing the footage later on that night,

Matt found himself watching that section again and again, aghast at how someone could simultaneously appear so streetwise and yet be so inarticulate. It was to be another scene he would remember for a long, long time.

Back on the stand-up circuit, David and Matt had started competing with each other as they both fought to climb up the career ladder. After his double acts with Myfanwy, David had formed a new comedy partnership with another fellow student called Jason Bradbury – who would go on to become a television presenter and one of the country's leading technology journalists. The pair first went on stage at Clifton's Dome Bar as part of the David Icke and the Orphans of Jesus nights. They then travelled the comedy circuit together for nearly four years – first as The Dr Johnsons of This World before settling on a softer, more mainstream set-up called Bunce & Burner – frequently misspelled on posters as Buns or even Bums & Burner.

In the small world of comedy, they were forever bumping into faces from Bristol – and it was dog eat dog when they did. 'At the East London Comedy Café one night we beat Matt in the "best newcomer" competition,' says Jason proudly. And back in Bristol he and David were also making headway on both local radio and television. After endless cold-calling and letter-writing, they were commissioned to make a show for BBC Radio Bristol. It was called *Bunce & Burner Visit Interesting Places* and while the fee was appalling and the listener figures were woeful it gave them an impressive new line to write on their comedy CVs.

Following on from that, the pair faced a lot of friendly jealousy back at university when they got on a show called *Get Me Out of Here* on what was then called Westcountry Television. But, in a pattern that David was to become accustomed to for most of the next decade, these early breaks didn't translate into any lasting achievements. He and Jason weren't sure if they had enough confidence in Bunce & Burner as a long-term act and they didn't seem to be coming up with any alternative ideas or characters. So after a while David decided to go back out on his own. He wanted to take a break from live comedy work and get some experience in television instead. So he got on the phone and started spraying out application letters to anyone who might be able to offer him a break. Very few responses came back – though, because he had spread his net so widely, David was never out of work.

Anyone who saw any of the live or televised shows of the likes of Jack Dee, Lee Evans and Mark Thomas back in the mid-1990s might just remember a tall, fresh-faced warm-up man who tried to get everyone in the mood for the star turn. That was David. If you had watched a lot of kids' television around the same time, you would have seen his face several times as well – popping up in a variety of different shows, almost always in minor and forgettable roles.

Behind the scenes, he was also working flat out. He got a job writing jokes for the first non-drama shows that Ant and Dec filmed after leaving *Byker Grove*. But, while much of David's work did get used, it wasn't enough for him. What he wanted to do was to escape the writers' room and get on stage with the two young performers. To everyone's amusement on set, he was constantly trying to find ways to be written into a sketch and get on national television himself. After *The Ant and Dec Show*, he got promoted to script editor on two series of Steve Furst's *The Lenny Beige Variety Pack* (several other faces from Bristol were crowded into the studios for filming). He also played the nerd and wrote for Sky One's *Gamesworld* and got back into a few other kids' TV roles.

As part of his move into the professional entertainment world, David had also changed the spelling of his surname – due to the Equity ruling that no two performers in the union could have the same name (and years later he would show there were no hard feeling by trying to find the existing David Williams a role in *Little Britain*).

But was this convoluted career really going anywhere? Anyone who has made it in television says starting out can be an exhausting process. You never know when you might get some work or when you might be left out in the cold. You never know which show might succeed and which will disappear without trace. And all around you there are people who are already in the jobs you reckon you were born to do. It can be a relentless, depressing treadmill that most people ultimately fall from. Angry about the way things were working out, David nearly did just that. But, before he quit altogether, he decided to give stand-up comedy one more try. It was when he was planning a new act that he recognised Matt's name on the sign-up sheet of a tiny London club and David decided to stick around to see how the younger man was getting on. Matt had been on good form (as had the very noisy audience) and David bought him a drink when he came off the stage to congratulate him. After a while, the pair began reminiscing about the National Youth Theatre, dissecting the acts they had seen on stage that night and discussing the state of British television. And then they realised that it was closing time and they were pretty much alone in the bar. They both decided it was a good sign that they had talked for so long, without noticing the time or anything that had been going on around them. It showed they still connected, that their comedy antennae were still firmly tuned into the same stations.

'We should do an act together,' said Matt, half-embarrassed, as they exchanged numbers and headed their separate ways at the end of the evening.

'That would be great,' said David.

And, with those few words, the greatest comedy partnership of its generation was born.

CHAPTER 5

HARD KNOCKS ON THE STAND-UP CIRCUIT

Matt and David were to spend many more late nights talking about what sort of joint act they could do. Having watched each other in a variety of different performances since leaving the National Youth Theatre, both had a pretty good idea of their respective strengths and weaknesses. And both knew what sort of comedy they preferred.

What Matt also liked, nearly five years after they had first met, was the new spark of anger he saw in David's eyes. It was an anger that temporarily matched his own, and Matt was convinced it made for a passion that could shine through from a stage. Anger, they decided would be their unique selling point and the foundation stone of their new act. When they hit the circuit together, they wouldn't be taking any prisoners. Their language was going to be X-rated and their audiences were in for a shock.

'David was strange and brilliant back then and we were scarily blue together, very hostile, very fierce and very abrasive,' says Matt. 'Our act was vulgar and juvenile and we would defend our offensive brand of comedy to the hilt. We were gleeful in mocking those sorts of uptight people who would recoil in horror at the merest hint of a rude word. Of course, our use of bad language was utterly fucking gratuitous, but it was also liberating in the extreme. Swear words can get laughs and it was a hell of a lot of fun.'

What the pair took time to realise, however, was that it wasn't for everyone. Still pushing at any door that could open on to the full-time entertainment world, they freelanced as joke and script writers for a variety of television shows. But their constant swearing didn't always go down very well. 'When we did some days work on television, we would get reams of notes from beleaguered producers demanding rewrites because of the language. I, in particular, was outraged by their cheek. I would moan and groan vociferously at the idea of having to change "what works" and tone things down.'

But, after a while, Matt realised that what works is what sells — so the pair of them did try to keep things clean. 'We had to admit that we were too rude for television and a while after our first expletive-filled comedy routines we realised we had grown out of just being relentlessly blue anyway,' says Matt. 'We decided to try and write jokes instead.'

One of their first long-term joint acts was called Mash

and Peas. It was a project they worked on with friend Edgar Wright, who would one day give the men their first big-screen roles in the zombie/comedy film *Shaun of the Dead*, as well as directing a host of their other shows. Matt played Danny Mash while David was Gareth Peas and the pair slogged it out on the comedy circuit hoping for a big break. Amazingly enough, they seemed to have got one within just a year of creating the act.

The news came when they took the show to Edinburgh, on the very furthest fringes of the Fringe. As well as constant bickering, a big part of the Mash and Peas act consisted of references to popular television shows. Matt and David would play the roles of various presenters – often getting laughs by transplanting them into some extreme or unlikely situations. Some nights they acted out whole scenarios as their alter egos, while on others they simply invited the audience to take part in mock-ups of popular shows – always with a surreal comedy twist.

A minor buzz started to build up around the spoofs – and one evening a group of executives from fledgling Paramount Comedy Channel joined the audience. Fortunately, Matt and David were on form that night and after a series of meetings they got their first real break.

Paramount reckoned the vignettes could work on screen as well as on stage – and so *Spoofovision* was born. The idea was to begin each show with a bungled or interrupted joke, before mocking the popular television shows that they had lampooned in their live act. Their attention to detail, even when working on minuscule budgets and to impossible deadlines, was impeccable. In their sights were the likes of *Jackanory*, *Why Don't You?*, *Littlejohn* and *Bushell on the Box*, while David also added a great spoof of pre-scandal Michael Barrymore to the mix. What got them the most laughs, however, were their ideas of how traditional British shows could end up as nightmares if transferred insensitively on to American television (*Only Jerks and Horses* with its lost-in-translation 'nice jubbly' catchphrase was the best). In effect, the whole short series was a form of *Rock Profiles* about television shows – long before the music spoof had even been thought of.

Sitting in the editing suite making sure *Spoofovision* was ready for transmission, both Matt and David could hardly hide their excitement. OK, so the Paramount Comedy Channel wasn't exactly mainstream television, and the series was never going to make them rich. But even the smallest cheques were welcome at this stage in their careers and they both knew that Paramount was central to the stand-up and entertainment industry. People they knew, and people who mattered, all watched it. So their hopes were high that this early breakthrough would lead to bigger and better things.

Unfortunately for them, it didn't. The commissioning executives said they were pleased with the performances. But it turned out that the shows had only ever been seen as stop-gap fillers to be slotted in between the channel's other bigger shows. And, while all the right people may have been watching, none of them picked up the phone to say two great new talents had clearly been discovered. It was the same when the pair re-jigged and re-cut the shows and saw them sold to Channel Four as part of its 'Sitcom Weekend' in the summer of 1997. Five of the mini-comedies were shown between the main shows, but once more the phone stubbornly failed to ring with any follow-up commissions.

Sitting at home and trying to work out what to do next, Matt and David felt more than usually deflated. What bothered them the most was a feeling that they had been foolish to think they could break into the big time so quickly. The fact that the Paramount commission had come so soon after setting up their new act had made them think they were going to have it easy. But, as most of the next decade would prove, they couldn't have been more wrong. They had a lot more hard work to do before getting a second chance at fame.

Back on the low-rent comedy-club circuit, Matt and David tried to put it all down to experience and keep looking for another way up the comedy ladder. They also built up a reputation for having one of the toughest work ethics in the business. 'For every gig I did, Matt probably did 20,' says comedian Paul Putner, who worked with them on their original Mash and Peas routines. 'People don't realise how seriously both those guys take the business, or how hard they work.' What Paul would also discover, over the years, was just how loyal the pair were to their friends. He subsequently worked with them on almost every show they ever made – finally turning up, among many other roles, as the long-suffering Paul in *Little Britain*'s Fat Fighters.

With *Spoofovision* and the Sitcom Weekend behind them, Matt and David did get another weird new challenge when the comedy group Fat Les asked them to be in the video for 'Vindaloo', the unofficial England song for the 1998 World Cup. Fat Les were Blur's Alex James, artist Damien Hirst and actor and rival comedian Keith Allen, so it was heady company for the still star-struck Matt and David. The song made it to Number Two in the charts and drove football-mad Matt wild with excitement while leaving David totally cold. Two years later, they would be back again in the video for 'Jerusalem' – having a bit more fun, working with Damien Hirst again on the filming, but once more making next to no money and no real headway in their careers.

And, long before this, Matt and David had already decided that Mash and Peas had probably gone as far as they could go. The excitement of writing new material for the characters wasn't keeping them awake at nights any more, and their minds had already started to move on to other characters and formats. So, instead of carrying on without any real conviction, they felt they should retire the act and focus full-time on something else. And fortunately they had another option waiting in the wings. Way back when they had first taken Mash and Peas to Edinburgh, they had decided to double up their workload and dust down Sir Bernard Chumley as well. And it turned out that he started to thrive, just as the other act started to die.

Looking back, it is clear that what gave Sir Bernard his vital second wind (quite literally, as bodily functions made up a large part of his increasingly over-the-top act) was the fact that Matt and David sat down to give him a far more detailed off-stage life before writing him any new material. It was a process that would stand them in good stead for all the comic creations that were still to come and would be an intrinsic part of their work ethic for the rest of their careers.

'We decided to base the new Sir Bernard more firmly on all the old theatrical raconteurs like Peter Ustinov and Ned Sherrin, as well as all those old fruits we used to find ourselves working with in youth theatre,' said David when they first began to detail the revamped act. 'I also wanted him based a little bit on how I intend to be in five years' time, sitting being appallingly rude to journalists in the Garrick over port and cigars.'

But, for all the savagery that would pour out of the character, David was also keen to emphasis a vein of sadness that the pair saw running through their man – a sadness that they felt gave Sir Bernard more weight and depth than the average sketch-show spoof. 'We have always been interested in people who are failures. There's something intriguing about people at their lowest ebb who refuse to admit it or face up to it. That is who we are fascinated by and that's who we tried to recreate on stage,' he said.

Matt, meanwhile, was starting to add more context by writing a list of all the part-time jobs their character had accepted over the years to try and make ends meet while waiting for his next big theatrical break. 'He's been a short-order chef, a waiter and a washer-up at the Wimpy in Hemel Hempstead,' he decided. 'Sir Bernard is very real. He has been very ill treated and he has decided that the profession is going to pay.'

With Sir Bernard himself fully fleshed out, the next task was to beef up his line-up and give David a chance in the spotlight as well. A host of cameo characters were created to introduce and work with the big man on stage, each with increasingly detailed back histories of their own.

The rewriting process was at its most intense when the pair shared a flat in Edinburgh for a month in 1995. The hurly burly of preparations for the Festival was going on all around them and each say it was an important time for both their personal and professional lives. 'Writing a show, and performing and living together means you are very much in each other's pockets every hour of the day,' says Matt, who admits tensions could have got out of control with almost anyone else. But with David the experience was entirely enjoyable. They worked hard, but were happy to put in whatever hours it took to get the act right. From the start, they found ideas bounced off each other very well – and they rekindled any of the enthusiasm for the business they had lost when previous projects had gone astray.

That first summer in Edinburgh they decided to call their revamped show *Sir Bernard Chumley is Dead... And*

Friends. The poster for it featured Matt as Sir Bernard in his full 'chummy old man' regalia (which included Matt's childhood wig) while David was perched on the arm of his leather chair unaccountably dressed only in underwear and sunglasses straight out of a 1970s cop show. And as the double entendres mounted up, the cast of friends in question turned out to be a fantastic group – the kind Victoria Wood could only ever have created if she were on acid.

David played Eric Estrada, a porn actor from Bristol, who related tales from the set of *That's Life! The Adult Movie* featuring Gavin 'he gets hard and he stays hard' Campbell, the inevitable Doc Cox, plus some girl-on-girl sex between Esther Rantzen and Mollie 'this time I really do mean my pussy' Sugden. Subtle it wasn't.

In the main act, Sir Bernard had also been taken up a gear. More malevolent than ever, he alternately whispered and then shouted at the audience while getting laughs and groans in equal measure for his lines about 'accidentally shitting on Felicity Kendall in rep' or 'trying to enter the Young Musician of the Year'. What the pair did do well was the writing. They had worked out exactly how a character such as Sir Bernard would talk – and then added some typically surreal elements to his anecdotes. 'Ah, how I remember *Babes in the Wood* with Sue Pollard, Ian McKellen and Ice-T. He had all the young boys up on stage singing "Cop Killer". What a gloriously innocent night that was...' being the start of one of the very few reprintable of Sir

Bernard's early stories. 'In 1974, I did a poo. In 1975, I did a wee…' was the start of another, as Sir Bernard ran through what he saw as his invaluable contribution to the heritage of the Fringe.

For a long time, most audiences just didn't get it, however. The act was heckled badly and, depending on the audience's mood and alcohol levels, it could be booed off stage or received in near-perfect silence. Neither Matt nor David can say which of these two reactions they hated or feared the most. 'We had to start off doing the show at midnight because that was the only slot we could get and, by that time, people were so pissed that it was basically a battle between us and them,' says David. 'At our first venue, the only way people could get to the toilet was by walking across the stage, and there was a constant procession because people were so pissed. But in the end we kind of incorporated all that into the act, which worked pretty well. It ended up as a great introduction to live comedy up there.' Everything about Edinburgh taught the pair important lessons, David says. 'You don't start off great in any business, especially this one. You have to make mistakes. And you need to learn from them. That's what we tried to do right from the start.'

Unfortunately for audiences of a more sensitive disposition, however, the worse the reaction the pair got while up on stage, the worse their language tended to become. 'I keep a count of how many times Matt says the c-word,' said David, backstage at that first Edinburgh

Festival in 1995. 'We try to have a ceiling of about three or four. But on one of the first nights he said it about 20 times and I have to admit that it started to lose its impact a bit.'

Matt's sudden lashings out at the audience ('I'll fuckin' 'ave you!' his Sir Bernard would scream, mid-anecdote and a propos nothing, at someone in the front row) were equally disconcerting as he veered from genteel luvvie to stark raving lunatic in the blink of a wet rheumy eye. And most nights the audience were already on edge by the time Matt hit the stage. As the pair honed the act, David's warm-up routine had became equally savage – he would rip latecomers to shreds, for example, attacking the clothes they were wearing, their appearance or their faltering replies to his increasingly offensive questions. Overall, it was a highly stressed night for the performers and the audience alike.

Matt and David had two key goals that first summer in Edinburgh – and one impossible dream. Goal number one was to play a bigger venue and get a better time slot. Goal number two was to get some decent press coverage and possibly even a slot on a television review show. The impossible dream was to catch the eye of some of the Perrier Award judges and at least get short-listed for a prize.

Over the years, the pair did meet their first goal. They played everywhere from the Gilded Balloon and the Pleasance Courtyard and Dome to the Assembly Rooms, and gradually managed to shake off their late-night spots and get themselves on stage at a more mainstream hour.

The pair met their second goal as well, rising above some of the estimated 16,000 performers and 1,800 shows to attract several top journalists to their audience – though some of the early reviews were ambivalent at best. 'Sodomising, sadistic and at times intimidatingly vengeful in a world of nightmarish childishness,' was how the *London Evening Standard* saw Sir Bernard that first summer, while refusing to say if he was a hit or a miss.

Fortunately, some other papers would soon decide to go with the hit, though. 'The sad old queen Sir Bernard Chumley is now clearly under the impression that he owns Edinburgh. So confidently does young Matt Lucas now inhabit his creation that Chumley stands to become the institution he imagines himself to be,' wrote the *Independent* in one of the very first good reviews that the pair cut out and kept.

'Lucas's performance is a joy to watch, switching from cherubic avuncularity to deranged alter ego with all the violence of radio interference. His blond wig, mischievous eyes, love of crude innuendo and physical catchphrases make him resemble that other self-knighted egomaniac Sir Les Patterson, albeit at the opposite end of the sexual spectrum,' the review continued.

Ah, Sir Les Patterson. From the start, both Matt and David had been terrified that their long-cherished character would seem like a rushed, copy-cat production of Barry Humphries's second stage act. The drinking, the bitterness, the anger, the awful clothes and the sheer physical dirtiness – the similarities were obvious. But, for all this, the boys were convinced that they had given their character the full and true off-stage life that could make him stand on his own two feet. And it did seem as if the critics and audiences were starting to agree.

As long as you didn't blink and miss it, you could see Sir Bernard on the BBC's *Edinburgh Nights* review show in 1995, which was just what Matt and David had hoped to achieve. And some of the bit-parts and warm-up roles that David had created were also getting a bit of press as well. They included a fiercely misogynist stage manager and a weirdly obsessed royal watcher, whom they hoped might one day be able to carry a show of his own.

But the one goal the pair didn't achieve in any of their three main seasons in Edinburgh was to really catch the eye of the Perrier judges. Jenny Eclair won the top comedy prize in their first season, 1995. Dylan Moran won in 1996, when Armstrong and Miller and Al Murray were on the shortlist, while the League of Gentlemen won in 1997, beating Graham Norton and Johnny Vegas to the prize.

Each year, Matt and David could only watch from the wings, hoping that their moment might still come. And each year, when the mad and manic Festival was over, the pair headed back down south with exceptionally mixed feelings about the experience. On the one hand, they always hoped some reflected glory from Edinburgh could boost their profile until they reached the next rung of the comedy ladder. But, on the other, there was always a sense of deflation. A feeling that another big opportunity might have passed them by – and that all the hard work and stress had been in vain.

'The comedy circuit is a very tough place to be,' says stand-up Michael Stansfield, who has been gigging around the country for more than a decade. 'The endless challenge is to keep your persona alive and fresh. And, however knackered or pissed off you are about your life or the industry as a whole, you know you have to be on form every night. You know that if you don't give it 100 per cent then that will be the night the commissioning editor or the producer will be in the audience with an open chequebook – and he'll close it because you don't look good enough. Talent scouts sound like something out of Hollywood in the 1930s. But their modern equivalents really do exist and as a comedian you spend your whole life just hoping one of them will see you – let alone like you.'

Sharing the same dream, Matt and David carried on trying to give 100 per cent as the comedy caravan moved off around the country again. And little by little they did seem to be catching the right people's eyes. The pre-revamp Sir Bernard had made very brief appearances on ITV's *Comedy Club* in 1993 and the *London Comedy Festival* in 1994. And the new improved version was about to get an even more unlikely gig. Following on from the Fat Les link with Mash and Peas, Blur's lead singer Damon Albarn had heard about the new character and came to a show with a group of friends. Sir Bernard, fortunately, was on top form. Going backstage to meet the boys afterwards, Damon promised to keep in touch and said he hoped they might be able to work together one day.

'Work with a rock group?' Matt and David couldn't imagine how they might pull it off, but, however it might happen, they were up for the challenge. And a couple of weeks later Damon rang them up with his proposal. Amazingly enough, he wanted Matt to play Sir Bernard in the Damien Hirst-directed video for 'Country House' – the song that would be one of the group's biggest-selling singles (though one they ultimately claimed to like the least). From then on, the professional relationship was mixed. On the positive front, Damon asked Matt (dressed as Sir Bernard) to go on stage and collect the Ivor Novello Award on his behalf when the singer was unable to attend the lavish ceremony. It was a night that gave the 21-year-old a first-hand and eye-watering view of life at the very top of the entertainment tree.

On the down side, however, Blur wanted Sir Bernard to go on the road with them on 1995's *Great Escape* seaside tour. At first, it sounded like it would be a great gig – and it offered pretty decent money for a change. But rock audiences and their teenybopper hangers-on didn't seem ready for camp comedy and their nightly reactions were brutal.

'All they wanted was to see Damon and they would scream, "Who's that fat bastard in the wig?" at me, so I would just get even more abusive and every night it just went downhill from there,' says Matt. Contracted to do a

30-minute set each night, he rarely managed more than 15. And as the tour went on he wasn't just being booed off stage – in Brighton, he had bottles thrown at him and was taken backstage for his own protection. 'Overall, the audience reaction ranged from sympathy to disgust via death threats,' he said years later, when he was able to laugh at it all. At the time, however, he admitted that the public rejection and humiliation was starting to hurt.

He and David would sit in the wings listening as Blur ran through their set after yet another stressful attempt to warm up the crowd. Not sure if they were banging their heads against a brick wall, the pair had to decide if this was what they really wanted to do, and where they really wanted to go.

'The very tough can slog it out in comedy for a lifetime, just ignoring the bad audiences, making a basic living and holding out some hope that they may one day make it big,' says Michael Stansfield. 'But most people give up at some point when they feel they're never going to really make it. Modern audiences at comedy clubs are far more brutal than they were in the past. They see it as part of the deal to heckle and give the performers hell, and you need to be committed, I think quite literally, to put up with it beyond a certain number of years.'

Michael says getting laughs and becoming popular isn't necessarily any guarantee that you can carry on doing the circuit either. 'If an act works, you can be forced to just stick with it gig after gig, which ultimately gets mind-numbingly boring. After a while, you start to look for other things just to keep your brain alive.'

For Matt and David, the 'other thing' in question was television, just as it always had been. They never gave up hope of getting their act back in front of the cameras on stage – and in 1996 they got the chance to take Sir Bernard on to the prime-time *Barrymore* show. More than ten million viewers would be watching, including all their peers in the entertainment industry. They both knew that this could be the biggest moment of their careers so far.

The show was filmed at the massive London Television Centre on the banks of the River Thames. It was big-budget, high-production stuff. And for all the excitement Matt and David were both terrified that they might blow it. Michael Barrymore, long before destroying his career with drunken outbursts, a body in his swimming pool and notorious news coverage turned out to be a strong supporter of new talent. 'I was only about 21 then and Michael was so generous to me in rehearsals,' says Matt. 'He would actually give me jokes to use and I don't know of any other comic who would do that to a rival, especially on his own show.'

With David working on scripts from the wings, Sir Bernard did his stuff in front of the cameras, ending up the act singing a bizarre duet with the show's star. And then – nothing. With hindsight, the men say their character was probably too off the wall and extraordinary for such a mainstream television show. There was also a sense that they had pushed the envelope a little bit too far and that their on-stage anger still needed to be controlled or focused rather than letting rip at anyone in their path. Attempting to verbally rip the host of the show apart as Sir Bernard had done had perhaps been a bad idea. The *Barrymore* producers did not ask them back. Once again, Matt and David felt they had reached a dead end. And they had no idea what to do next.

CHAPTER 6

SHOOTING STARS

Throughout all the relentless gigging with Mash and Peas and Sir Bernard Chumley, Matt in particular had hopes that a different project might one day give him a chance at the big time. It was a dream that had sustained him through his first year at Bristol University and had kept him going when the first comedy audiences were particularly brutal about his live act. And, when the dream finally turned into reality, it looked as if it might force him to leave David behind.

The opportunity came courtesy of his unexpected link to Bob Mortimer and Vic Reeves – and it would ultimately lead to the creation of George Dawes and *Shooting Stars*. The long, slow-burn process had begun back in 1992, just five weeks after Matt's first ever stand-up performance as an 18-year-old schoolboy. There hadn't been many people in the audience on the night in question, but one of them, Bob Mortimer, had thought he spotted real potential in the strange-looking young man on stage. At that time, Bob had been working for Jonathan Ross's Channel X and was one of the rising stars of British comedy. 'I thought Matt was the angriest man I had ever met,' he said when asked his impressions of the teenager's act. And he meant that as a compliment. The comedian went backstage (a cramped store-room near the club's staff toilets) in order to speak to Matt after the show.

'You were good,' he said honestly, and told Matt they should stay in touch.

As a huge fan of Channel Four's *Vic Reeves Big Night Out*, which had also showcased Bob's talents, Matt was over the moon. One of his comedy heroes hadn't just seen his act – he had liked it. More importantly, Matt was convinced he had made his first essential contact with the mainstream entertainment industry. All you ever need is a way in, he had always said, as he and David dreamed of making it big. When you get in, you can prove yourself and then you've got it sorted. Bob Mortimer, he was convinced, was ready to hold open the door for him.

Desperate not to let the contact go cold, Matt wrote to Bob, giving as much information as possible about what he thought he could offer any television show his hero might be working on. Bob wrote back and Matt says he treasured the letter for years – though in all this time the contact didn't really seem to be leading anywhere. Finally, at Bristol, Matt decided to try and get back in touch, though when he and Bob finally spoke on the phone Matt says he thought he might actually pass out with nerves and excitement. 'I ended up making a phone call to Bob Mortimer of all people from a payphone at the Bristol Student Union. Even now I can't really take that in,' he said years afterwards. 'Speaking to him felt like the beginning of a shift from not being part of a world to being part of it and it was fantastic.'

Except, of course, for the fact that the renewed contact still failed to lead anywhere. At that point, Bob was just networking and he had no firm work ideas for the angry young stand-up with the dodgy wig and the dirty mouth. So Matt went back to his studies and his stand-up. A mammoth waiting game was about to begin.

In 1992, Bob and Vic were about to start work on *Weekenders* for Channel Four and *At Home With Vic and Bob* for BBC2. Their production teams were happy to take calls from the likes of Matt and David and would even pay them if they came up with any decent jokes or formats. But regular onscreen work was out of the question. Matt, meanwhile, tried signing up with a variety of agents to try and push himself forward, saying he would be available for acting, singing and voice-over work as well as advertising, radio, television or film jobs. He sent letters to as many producers or television company executives as he could find and kept on writing as many sketches and jokes of his own in the hope that one day they might see the light of day.

What he didn't always focus on as much was his academic work – and university was pretty much forgotten altogether one day when Bob called him up out of the blue in order to set up an informal audition. 'Imagine sitting in a bedsit in Bristol trying to write an essay when you are meeting Vic Reeves and Bob Mortimer at the weekend,' he said of that extraordinary week when the meeting was looming over him. And this time Vic and Bob did come through. They wanted Matt to play some bit parts on the new show they were taking from Channel Four to BBC2 – *The Smell of Reeves and Mortimer*. Matt leaped at the chance – and began a working relationship that would last for the next eight years – and a friendship that survives to this day.

Being a small part of *The Smell of Reeves and Mortimer* was an extraordinary experience for Matt – who was easily the youngest person on the team. It was a ground-breaking (and for Bob and Vic, career-building) show. At its peak it got more than six million viewers – no mean feat for BBC2 – and a comedy cult seemed to have begun. But as far as its two stars were concerned it was only the beginning. They had an even more bizarre show ready to roll – *Shooting Stars*.

The pilot show was aired in 1993 with Jonathan Ross and Danny Baker as team captains and an unlikely cast, including Martin Clunes, Noddy Holder and Wendy Richards, trying to work out what the hell was going on. The producers loved the result and the audience reaction was good. But Vic and Bob felt there was something missing. If they were to do a full series, they wanted things to be that little bit more surreal. And they thought they knew just the man to help them.

'I was back at Bristol and one day Bob rang me up and described the show to me. He said, "You're George Dawes. You're a big baby. You play the drums. Make it up as you go along." For ages afterwards, I said it was all very spontaneous. But in reality it was all pretty shambolic,' says Matt of the way he was invited to join the revamped *Shooting Stars* cast. Billed as: 'the quiz of the business we call show', Mark Lamarr and Ulrika Jonnson were subsequently drafted in to replace Jonathan and Danny as team captains. Mark was a rising star of the comedy circuit and his 1950s quiff would be a standing joke on the series. Ulrika, famous as the ambitious Swedish weather girl from TV-am, was trying to win a new, edgier fan base. The show was a big deal for both of them. But, as shooting began, neither was as nervous as Matt.

The problem wasn't the fact that the programme was recorded in front of a live studio audience in London – Matt of all people was used to working in front of a crowd. What confused him was the stop–start process of making a big-budget television show. Whole packs of producers and assistant producers seemed to be darting around or giving the leads instructions through their headsets. Everyone seemed to know exactly what they were doing – and, as someone who had almost always been on stage on his own, Matt found it hard to fit in with such an ensemble production. He had also failed to appreciate just how much footage was left on the cutting-room floor each week. At the start, as much as three hours of studio time could be used to film each half-hour show. The odds of him getting a big scene were low.

The *Shooting Stars* format was deliberately bizarre. Among other things, teams tried to build up a pot of money by answering questions and performing unlikely tasks. Graham Skidmore ('our Graham' from *Blind Date*) did the voice-overs and catchphrases abounded – including the 'Dove from Above' (some weeks replaced by 'The Crow from Below', 'The Vest from the West', or 'The Beast from the East'). Each week, Bob would smash Vic over the head with a giant frying pan, every female guest was flirted with outrageously, and entertainment giants were shamelessly ridiculed. Jarvis Cocker being told to throw mini Baby-Bel cheeses at a life-size cardboard cut-out of Judy Finnigan was a particular favourite – especially as he was told to throw them 'in the style of a girl'.

Matt's big moment was to read out the scores as each quiz round ended – to a cry of 'What are the scores, George Dawes?' from the show's hosts.

As Bob had told him in the original phone call, Matt would be speaking from behind a drum kit (his own – the one given to him by his grandmother on his bar mitzvah). And, as Bob had also suggested, he would be dressed as a baby. 'They wanted me to wear a nappy but I said at first I would only do it in a blue romper suit,' he claims when asked about the costume choice. 'But when it came from wardrobe the suit was pink. And there was a rattle.'

At first, however, it looked as if the colour of his suit would be the brightest thing about Matt's role. Under pressure from the start, his jokes dried up, his timing seemed to have failed and for the first two programmes he failed to raise a single laugh from the studio audience. 'The first couple of shows are just me yelling. None of the gags I told made the final edit. The audience was just there to see Reeves and Mortimer and I was just an irrelevance,' he admits. But suddenly, in show three, Matt took a chance.

'The next time I was asked the scores, I just said, "So, you want to know the scores then, you fat cow," at Ulrika Jonnson. I said it straight down the lens. And it got a huge laugh. Suddenly George Dawes had a bit of attitude. And from then on I started to take on the stars themselves. I would ask Griff Rhys Jones, "Have you seen *Pretty Woman*?" And he would go, "Yeah," and I would go, "So have I. What's the big deal? It's on video, it's been on television. What, are you trying to be the big man here?" And it seemed to keep getting laughs.'

George Dawes became a cult hit. Matt's one-liners were to become as surreal as Vic and Bob had hoped – 'Doris! Get that Eccles cake out of your arse, our children must eat! Mark has Four, Ulrika has Five,' being just one typically bizarre piece of score-keeping. Matt also revelled in the extraordinary group of stars he was suddenly getting the chance to meet. On the show's first series, he worked with everyone from John Peel, Peter Stringfellow, Chris Rea and Shane Ritchie to Muriel

Gray, Leslie Ash, Chris Evans and Martine McCutcheon. Cries of 'He's a baby! He's a baby!' and 'What's the scores, George Dawes?' started to follow him down the street back in Bristol and, while the idea of making a living dressed as an overgrown baby might not appeal to everyone, Matt realised that for the first time in many years he was happy. He had a foot in the door of a world he loved – and he had a bizarre feeling of affection for the character who had got him there and the freedom that he engendered.

'George was a great character because you'd never know what was going to happen next with him. People used to say to me, "How can you put on that babygro? Don't you feel ridiculous?" Well, I obviously felt ridiculous meeting guests in hospitality in a big pink suit, but once you put it on you could get away with a lot more because you were clearly not setting yourself up as pompous. If you're subsumed by a character, you're more likely to do extraordinary things. Look at Dame Edna. Barry Humphries would never get away with those insults, but in Edna's voice criticising someone is funny. Making a total fool of yourself is actually very liberating. You can't have any vanity in comedy and, when you have run around in front of millions dressed as a baby, you're not too scared of failure any more,' he pointed out at the time.

And, as the show slowly found its feet, Matt found he wasn't alone in being asked to don a bizarre costume. David was also signed up for a host of cameo roles –

including that of Soft Alan 'the biggest fruit in the world'. You had to see it to understand it, as they say.

The BBC realised that it had a hit on its hands with *Shooting Stars* and quickly signed everyone up for a Christmas special and a 14-episode second series. Matt knew as he looked at the contract that his drama course was going to have to go on hold – though persuading his family that he should take a year out of university wasn't as easy. 'My mum said, "I'm not sure you're making the right decision" and I admit it did seem strange to be telling her, "I'm giving up university to be a baby and bang drums." She just didn't get it. But my dad said, "Go for it." So I did. The biggest career risk to me at that point seemed to be staying at Bristol and that's the way it turned out.'

That one-year sabbatical would ultimately turn into a permanent absence. Matt never went back to Bristol to complete his degree. But, when your show is collecting a host of Bafta awards as well as the Silver Rose at the Montreux Festival, as *Shooting Stars* did in 1996, you can be excused for thinking academia can go on hold. Matt stayed with Vic and Bob on *Shooting Stars* for three seasons (and came back for a fourth series in 2002 when most of the original team re-formed).

The group also did a couple of hugely successful tours. They first went on the road in 1996 and two years later they teamed up with *The Fast Show* to play a record-breaking 30 nights at the Hammersmith Apollo (more than The Beatles, Michael Jackson or The Rolling Stones had done at that venue). In total, *Shooting Stars* was seen by an estimated 135,000 people in the course of that five-week run. It was heady stuff, especially for Matt, who was still in his early twenties. But for all the applause and the interest (and for all the people with his face on their T-shirts) Matt was coming to realise that he was just a bit-player on the big stages, and that the real stars were still his teenage heroes Vic and Bob. 'For me, it was just B-list fame,' he said of George Dawes. And even at the height of the show's success Matt was earning just £450 per show. It was a regular income and more than he had ever made before. But it was hardly enough to let him feel much confidence in his future – so he still worried he had made a mistake leaving Bristol without a formal qualification.

Matt was also starting to feel claustrophobic behind the drum kit, despite being given more songs to sing and a slightly bigger role in every show (he introduced George Dawes's mother Marjorie as a character, though his brilliantly named father Jack Dawes ended up on the cutting-room floor). 'In the end I did used to get frustrated because I knew I was capable of so much more,' he said as the third series of the show drew to a close. 'Career-wise it is hard to know how much further you can take a baby on the drums.'

Fortunately, Matt wasn't the only one to spot the intrinsic limitations in the romper-suited role. *Shooting Stars* mega-fan Lydia Ball says she could always tell Matt was holding something back – and would one day be given the right platform from which to release it. 'Everyone on the show was hilariously funny at one point or another, though you could tell that many of the good lines had been pre-written and rehearsed to sound like off-the-cuff comments. Somehow, though, you could always sense that in real life Matt Lucas was the funniest and the cleverest of all of them. He seemed to have the driest and the fastest sense of humour, like he was always feeling the way the room was going and was ready to come up with something extra to move the humour on. But you also got the feeling that he had to keep this kind of thing in check most of the time because he didn't have the chance to take control. The format of the show meant no single performer could really shine and I think he lost out most of all because of it.'

Other people had also seen Matt's potential after the first few *Shooting Stars* shows had been filmed – though the biggest role he was offered back then was hardly on the cutting edge of comedy cool. His bald head had caught the eye of the creative team putting together a series of new 'How do you eat yours?' adverts for Cadbury's Creme Eggs. Matt signed up because, while the script wasn't exactly Shakespeare, the job did offer three key benefits. First, as a self-confessed chocoholic, it made him feel, quite literally, like a kid in a candy store. Secondly, the money was better than he was earning on *Shooting Stars*. Finally, even his mother approved. 'It was only when I got the Creme Eggs job that my mum felt

I had done the right thing by giving up on my degree. If you are in an advert people assume you are making loads of money and this allayed her fears about my future,' he says.

The role certainly got Matt noticed, as well – though this wasn't always a good thing. 'Aren't you that weird bald bloke from the chocolate advert?' he was constantly asked in the street, never quite sure how he was expected to reply. Having spent a lifetime being mocked about his appearance, Matt says he should have been ready for the new onslaught. But, when *loaded* magazine sandwiched him between Buddha and Gary Glitter in its 'Fat Bald Blokes All-Time Top Ten' chart, he had to admit his fragile self-esteem took a bit of a knock. As it did years later when Jonathan Ross joked that the first time they had met on the set of *Shooting Stars* he had thought Matt was a ill child wanting a 'meet a celebrity' moment.

Vic and Bob continued to be incredibly supportive of their strange-looking protégé, however. They had an incredibly loyal team of collaborators on their shows (just as Matt and David would when their joint careers finally kicked off) so Matt was given several onscreen and behind-the-scenes roles on everything from the *It's Ulrika* sketch show in 1997 through *Bang Bang It's Reeves and Mortimer* in 1998 to *Randall & Hopkirk Deceased* in 2001. But, throughout all this, Matt was desperate to make a breakthrough of his own. Right from the start, he and his agent had constantly been seeking out new opportunities

– ideally, those that wouldn't require him to wear a nappy or resemble a piece of confectionery.

One role that did neither – but was still typically weird – was as a disturbing, if not downright disturbed, farmer in the short BBC2 series *Sunnyside Farm*. 'A character who seems all country warmth and old-fashioned values but, underneath, is a cross-dressing sexual deviant' was how the BBC described the part. In 1997, the show won itself a fantastic Friday-night slot at 9.30pm on BBC2, but the six episodes largely disappeared without trace. Critics said it was memorable only for its almost total lack of likeable characters.

Fortunately, Matt hadn't had any problems fitting in the filming schedule for *Sunnyside Farm* around his commitment to *Shooting Stars*. When it got going, the sketch show took a surprisingly small amount of time to make – several episodes were filmed in the same week, if not on the same day. And, once the series was finished, up to a year could pass before the green light was given for a follow-up.

It all meant Matt had plenty of time for other projects – which was why he and David put so much time and effort into Mash and Peas and Sir Bernard Chumley in his downtime. Years later, when *Little Britain* exploded into the mainstream, many commentators would give Matt and David the clichéd label of 'overnight sensations'. In reality, they had been plugging away and paying their dues for nearly a decade – often in the performance wilderness. And, while Matt had initially had the highest profile of the pair, there were times when it seemed David might race up on the inside and overtake him.

The first hint of the role-reversal came in 1998 when an extraordinary group of people were pulled together by Channel X to produce *Barking*. It was billed as '25 writer-performers do 135 sketches in 58 locations' – and it got a six-episode summertime run on Channel Four. Matt and David were both on board, alongside the likes of Marcus Brigstocke, Mackenzie Crook and Catherine Tate. As usual, it was a great chance to shine and David's portrayal of the desperate royal watcher – first created as a part of the warm-up to the Sir Bernard Chumley live shows and ultimately revived in *Little Britain* – was seen as a star turn of the series. Matt's roles, however, all sank without trace and the show itself was widely seen to have bombed. 'A mountain of mediocrity', 'a disjointed circus' and 'utterly puerile and almost entirely unfunny stuff', as three reviewers concluded. *Barking* was neither recommissioned nor repeated and everyone involved seemed keen to forget all about it.

As usual, Matt and David were determined to learn something from the experience, however. They still believed in the sketch-show format and they still loved creating larger-than-life characters. What they needed was the proper platform on which to present them. After the 'cast of thousands' structure of *Barking*, Matt and David had also realised that they worked better as a duo than as part of an ensemble writing factory. Their sense of humour still gelled and they were ready to commit to writing together for the long term. Almost all their comedy heroes, past and present, worked in pairs. So, as their other work dried up, Matt and David went back to the drawing board.

CHAPTER 7

A NEW ACT

'I couldn't write comedy with my best friend,' says London stand-up Lloyd Pierce, who saw Matt and David perform in the late 1990s. 'If he got less laughs than me I'd think he wasn't pulling his weight and I'd want to kill him. If he got more laughs than me I'd think he was undermining me and I'd want to kill him. If he got the same number of laughs as me I'd probably think I didn't really need him any more and I'd want to kill him. I'd say a pattern is starting to emerge there. Which is why I write my own material on my own. It might not be the easiest way to do it, but it's a lot less messy than the alternative. And ultimately it saves a lot of police time.'

In the late 1990s, Matt and David still thought working as a partnership was a risk worth taking – though most of their contemporaries would have said the pair had far more pulling them apart than they had holding them together. At first glance, it certainly seems true that the men are utterly different – not for nothing would they so often be called the odd couple of comedy.

One of the most obvious of the potentially divisive issues for them is football. Matt says it has always obsessed him and it is often all he wants to talk about. David simply couldn't care less about it. 'When my dad was 15, he had a bike accident and the doctor who repaired his smashed legs was the Arsenal team doctor,' is how Matt describes falling in love with the game – and the Gunners in particular. 'The doctor gave my dad some Arsenal tickets and it became a family thing from then on.'

As a teenager, Matt's football mania got him a Saturday job at Wembley Stadium – though, instead of getting to watch matches for free as planned, he says that most of the time he was told to go out with a dustpan and brush to clean up the manure from the police horses. His other footballing claim to fame as a teenager was that he got a job in Chelsea's shop, though as an Arsenal fan he says he always wore a red strip under the blue Chelsea shirt he was forced to wear on match days. One day during his 11-month stint there (he ended up as assistant manager), he took a bizarre phone call from the *Sun* newspaper. Apparently, they wanted a Chelsea shirt to photograph for some sort of promotion. Without being told any more, Matt packed one up and sent it off – and a week later he saw actress Antonia de Sancha wearing it as part of her infamous David Mellor kiss-and-tell story.

Years later, football still dominated Matt's thoughts. In the autumn of 2003, a newspaper published his answers to its regular 'celebrity questions', for example. And for the living person he most despised he ignored the usual choices of Margaret Thatcher, Tony Blair, Saddam Hussein or George W Bush and replied, 'Ryan Giggs, for scoring that goal,' referring to the Manchester United star's extra-time goal that defeated Arsenal in the 1999 FA Cup semi-final.

A subsequent question in the interview was: 'Which words or phrases do you most overuse?' He replied, 'I. Hate. Sir. Alex. And: Ferguson.'

A theatre journalist also got brought up short when Matt's football focus seemed to get in the way of their interview later that year. 'What's your ambition for the future?' he was asked.

'Apart from playing for Arsenal?' Matt replied.

'Yes, apart from that.'

'And apart from seeing Arsenal play more decent football?'

'Yes, apart from that as well.'

'Can't think of anything at all.'

Talking football trivia, which Matt likes to do almost endlessly, is not an option with David, however. Having admitted that he prefers the company of women and that he feels he 'doesn't have a lot to share' with other men, David says football talk is his least favourite pastime. 'My heart sinks when I get into a taxi and someone starts talking to me about football,' he says. 'The other week I was walking into a car park, and coming out was someone I recognised. It was a famous person, the guy who is married to the pop star Louise Nurding – Jamie Redknapp. He saw me and said, "Hey, well done on the comedy awards last night, mate, well deserved." And I instantly thought, OK, now I have to pay him a compliment back. But I was at a loss. Does he still play football? And, if so, who for? Has he scored recently? What do I say? So, I said, "Keep kicking those balls!" And in this absolutely tragic way I felt like such a failure.'

And when it comes to saying the wrong thing about football, David already had form. 'The worst thing David has ever said to me was when Arsenal got knocked out of the semi-final of the FA Cup by Manchester United in 1999,' remembers Matt. 'I came in the next day feeling really glum and told Dave they had lost and he just looked up and said, "Well, that's because they weren't good enough." It wounded me in the heart and I've never forgotten it.'

Away from the football pitch, other more obvious differences between Matt and David have always been there, and would become more pronounced as the years went by. For a start, there has always been Matt's gayness versus David's '70 per cent heterosexuality' – of which more later.

Always there, but getting more noticeable over time, was the contrast between Matt's shy domesticity and David's clear love of London's late-night celebrity circuit. Fashion or love of clothes hardly bring the pair together either – David admits to a lifelong love of designers and dressing up, while Matt couldn't dress further down if he

96

tried. When their careers took off and David had money to burn, he would spend small fortunes on bespoke Savile Row suits and would ultimately end up in several 'most fashionable men in Britain' lists. At the very few parties or interviews he ever attends, Matt, meanwhile, tends to be the figure at the back of the room with a baseball cap pulled down over his eyes, wearing old jeans, tatty trainers and a baggy sweatshirt (though, after relentless exposure to David's sartorial influence, he did also end up buying a Savile Row jacket when *Little Britain* first became a hit – and said it was something he should have done years ago).

Travel hasn't brought the pair together, either – Matt is a nervous flier and has always resisted buying a car in London. David is happy to get on a plane at the drop of a passport and says going on *Top Gear* was one of the best things about finally becoming a celebrity. Their homes have always illustrated yet another big difference between the pair (Matt's is 'always in a mess' while David's is 'all tarted up like Liberace's holiday home'). And yet still the pair spend around eight hours a day alone together, holed up in one or other of their flats with pads of paper and computers trying to turn themselves into a modern-day Morecambe and Wise, Dick Emery or The Two Ronnies. For putting all their differences aside, the six-foot-three David and five-foot-six-and-a-half Matt both say they have never met anyone else who shares their total devotion to classic television comedy – or to today's popular culture. Both admit they can happily spend hours watching *GMTV*, *Trisha* and *This Morning* ('I've learned everything I need to know about life by midday,' jokes David). And afterwards they can discuss what they have seen for almost as long.

Looking back, they have an encyclopaedic knowledge of comedy sketch shows and formats from the past and say they can again discuss them well into the night. Both say they seem to instinctively know, and to agree on, what works in comedy and what doesn't. This shared love of mainstream television goes right back to their respective childhoods. 'For me, Christmas has always been about the television,' says Matt. 'When I was a kid I would type up my entire viewing schedule. I would then calculate how many videotapes I needed and which show would go on what tape. I was frighteningly thorough.' The same was true of telly-obsessed David.

The television connection goes back all the way to their days at the National Youth Theatre, when they first watched rising stars Vic and Bob in *Vic Reeves Big Night Out*. 'It was probably like previous generations of music fans seeing the Sex Pistols,' David says of the way the pair sat, open mouthed and with tears of laughter running down their faces. 'We were both hooked and, while everyone else seemed to love the shows as well, no one else seemed to become as obsessed as we both did.' No one else talked about them quite so long afterwards, or were still doing so more than five years later, either.

What also keeps the pair working together (and not killing each other as rival comedian Lloyd Pierce might have predicted) is the simple fact that they enjoy the process of the job. Even before they knew they had a show in which they could put them, both say they got a huge buzz out of creating characters, scenarios and structures. They also like the relatively solitary way in which they choose to work – the two of them together in a room bouncing ideas off each other for as long as it takes to raise a laugh. In America in particular, big comedy shows tend to be written by committee, often in offices where teams of writers and others all pitch in with scenarios and jokes. Back in the late 1990s, after the debacle of *Barking*, Matt and David both decided they didn't want to go down that route. And they have tried to stay true to the decision ever since.

In those early days of their professional partnership there was even more pressure on the pair, not least because they were earning very little money and had no idea if they were ever going to make a breakthrough. But while the odds of them falling out were high the pair stayed friends through good times and bad. Even Matt's success on *Shooting Stars* didn't affect their equilibrium. David would often help his friend with jokes or songs for the show and attended many of the recording sessions to offer moral support from the wings. Both say they always felt that individual projects may sometimes lift one of them temporarily above the other. But both agreed that they should keep things in perspective and head back to their respective kitchens to write as a duo during any downtime. At this point in their careers, their friendship was already one of the strongest in the business.

'I think all double acts have moments of tension,' says Matt, when asked about the long hours they spend working together. 'But I don't think we have ever had a real falling out. There haven't been any drunken rows, though there's been the odd sober one every six months or so. We've got broadly the same political beliefs, though we don't tend to get into huge political conversations.'

'Right back from the start people seem to have been looking for the cracks in our friendship,' says David. 'But to be honest we struggle to find them ourselves.'

And in the early days of their writing partnership the pair did go through some particularly testing times – not least when Matt's father John died suddenly of a heart attack aged just 52.

Always close to his dad, even during the four years John had spent in prison, the 22-year-old Matt was devastated. 'It was traumatic and it affected Matt very much because he was so close to his father,' his mum admitted afterwards.

In some ways, comedy – and role-playing – got Matt through the darkest times. 'I had to do a gig nine days after my dad died, when being human was hard enough and obviously you just don't feel funny at all,' he said later. 'And I found there is a satisfaction in technique, even when you can't muster the energy.'

Matt also found that David was a true friend in that time of crisis. They were continuing to juggle all their writing and performing roles with Matt's *Shooting Stars* work and David took on as much as possible to give his friend time to recover. 'He supported me enormously,' Matt remembers. From then on a new level of joint respect would further underpin their friendship.

On a lighter note, the pair say their writing and performance partnership has also survived because of the obvious differences between them. 'We've got a lot of shared tastes, but we have totally different worlds,' Matt says. 'David's a great deal more cultured than me: he goes to art galleries, I'm much happier in front of the telly. That means that between us we know about everything, which is a pretty nice position to be in.'

David agrees that the pair's differences are in some ways what keep them together rather than what drives them apart. 'If you are going to write well with someone then I think you actually need to be different from them. Matt comes up with ideas I would never have thought of, and hopefully vice versa. It's a good partnership but writing is so intense, just the two of us, every day in each other's house, so I think it is important to go and do something else at night and at weekends. And I think it is good for all the shows and for our friendship that we have quite different interests.'

Their lack of ego, and the fact that they were both prepared to let others take the glory for the good of their shows, was another fact that made their working relationship so stable. This came to the fore in one of the first projects they tackled after being on *Barking*, and while they were still trying to get Sir Bernard Chumley a regular television slot. The project had first taken shape when both men, along with the rest of the country, had followed the hysteria of Take That's split, and had seen how the boy-band crown had moved almost seamlessly to Boyzone, then Westlife and then a host of other seemingly disposable pop acts.

Surely there is a story there, they thought, sitting as usual around David's kitchen table in north London with notepads at the ready. Surely this is a subject ripe for a proper parody? And so, after a lot of writing and rewriting, *Boyz Unlimited* was born. Matt and David came up with the idea of Nigel Gacey, a cockney wide-boy who reckons boy bands could be his next best get-rich-quick scheme. In the Lucas/Williams imagination, Nigel (whose first name may seem familiar to Take That fans) became a borderline-deranged pop svengali figure who puts an advert in *The Stage* newspaper to try and find the ingredients for a perfect band. He ends up with a singer/songwriter called Gareth, whom he describes as 'a fat boy who writes the music' (no prizes for guessing which performer he might have been based on). And no prizes either for spotting the real-life templates for Scott 'the cute one', Little Nick 'the even more cute one' and Jason 'the other one' who also line up in front of Nigel for the audition process.

With the scripts almost written, Matt and David set about trying to get the show made – and straight away they found some pretty powerful backers. Denise O'Donoghue, soon to set up the massively successful Hat Trick production company, signed up to produce *Boyz*

Unlimited − and she wanted the job done fast. The idea was to record the show by the end of 1998 so it could be shown over six weeks in the spring of 1999 while the boy-band theme was still hot. Casting took place straight away and as there were no roles for Matt or David they stood by ready to polish the scripts or write any additional material as required. Both say it was yet another useful learning experience to be entirely off-camera in one of their shows. But once again they also say it was a show that promised much but never really got them anywhere.

On a positive front, one early reviewer said scripts did manage to squeeze 'a little bit more out of what could have been a one-joke wonder', which was flattering. Another review sent a few warning bells ringing, however − and as the show had hardly set the ratings alight Matt and David knew it was something that they had to address.

At issue was the description of the show as a 'cynical and savage attack' on the modern pop world. The critic said the writing was more aggressive than comic − which was the last thing Matt and David wanted to be told. Their aim had never been to write the sort of politically aware satire of *Bremner, Bird & Fortune* − they just wanted to make people laugh. So back in West Hampstead, where Matt and David talked through yet another lengthy post-mortem on the programme, they decided it might be time to lighten up.

Producer Nira Park, who had worked with them a

couple of years earlier on the far softer reworked set of *Sit Com Spoofs* for Channel Four, was seen as the ideal person to help them do just that. Nira had just collected together an incredible group of comic talents for a one-off comedy drama to be called *You Are Here* – and after overcoming some initial reservations Matt and David signed up to join forces with them. The drawbacks, they felt, included the fact that they would be part of another ensemble exercise, this time as part of a four-strong lead writing team alongside Keith Allen and Paul Kaye.

The thing that persuaded Matt and David that they should go ahead was the fact that they thought they could learn a huge amount by working with the likes of Keith and Paul. They were also excited about the chance to work with cast members such as Nigel Planer and Kate Robbins. More importantly, the show's overall look and feel appealed to the boys' senses of humour. The setting was a chocolate-box-pretty village called Here, in which all sorts of bizarre goings on happened behind closed doors – a theme that both men had loved since their suburban childhoods. At the centre of Here would be a sinister family of alternative comedians, all of whom lived alongside what for Matt and David was already becoming a trademark group of oddballs and misfits. In equally trademark style, Matt's character was 'gender-confused' while David's was simply odious.

The show was great fun to make and as its characters came alive on the page Matt and David were convinced that they had found their form. *The League of Gentlemen*, to which Matt and David would one day be endlessly compared, had not yet seen the light of day. But in *You Are Here* its style was already on show. From the fey B&B proprietor and the endlessly camp vet to the fractured central family, Matt and David's influence in the show could be seen almost everywhere. This, they thought, was what they had been born to do – and they were devastated once again when they found out that the audiences and the critics didn't agree with them.

Unfortunately for everyone concerned, *You Are Here* was dismissed as a 'one-off curio piece' when it was ultimately broadcast in the dead week between Christmas and New Year's Eve in 1998. It was yet another of the boys' shows that was never recommissioned or repeated. And for many months that hurt them both badly.

As a result of this latest failure, neither of the men was particularly happy as Big Ben signalled the start of 1999. And, as the year got under way, things didn't improve. Their biggest worry was that *The League of Gentlemen* was on screen, and starting to do all the things Matt and David had dreamed of doing themselves, and they worried that they would no longer be called originals if they ever got the chance to follow suit. Both men felt they were still on the outside of the entertainment industry looking in. It was, they said, like being the comedy bridesmaids watching everyone else have a big white wedding. And it felt lousy.

What they wanted – and still very desperately needed – was a hit. But would it ever happen? In a rare moment of doubt, Matt decided to try and spread another safety net underneath him in case it didn't. He felt he needed a more regular source of income so he took on a private project that didn't get him anywhere at the time, but that would one day turn out to have been surprisingly prescient.

His project was to try and script a full half-hour episode of *EastEnders* in a bid to get a more secure writing job. Writing speculative scripts like this is a common way of breaking into this most competitive of markets and soap producers say they are always happy to read people's work and try and spot a new talent. The BBC in particular is keen to guide prospective writers so that they produce their best work. 'Try not to replicate something that has already hit the screens and try to make sure that everything you write is unique in some way,' it suggests in its 'writers' room' guidance notes. 'Try to hook the interest of the audience as soon as possible so they will want to stay tuned, and, if there are more episodes to come, they will want to keep tuning in,' it concluded.

Matt's script idea certainly aimed to do all of this. But it turned out the editors thought it was a little bit ahead of its time. Sitting at the keyboard in his north London flat, he decided to try and get noticed with an idea he didn't think anyone would expect. So he decided to resurrect Dirty Den, imagining somehow that the character could have survived the canal-side shooting of 1989 and was ready to head back to Albert Square as if he had never been away. Getting ready to post his script to the *EastEnders'* producers, Matt was sure he was in with a chance – not least because the Elstree Studios, where the soap is filmed, are in his native Borehamwood. Surely that has to be a good sign, he thought, as he dropped the package into the postbox.

But it didn't turn out that way. Matt's script ended up on the editor's 'slush pile' with all the other speculative work and was roundly rejected. A dead character like Dirty Den coming back to life? How ridiculous, the producers said, moving on to other things.

Funnily enough, Matt wasn't the only one potentially tinkering with a television classic in the late 1990s. David, a lifelong *Doctor Who* fan, had jumped at the chance to write and film three short spoof links for the BBC's *Doctor Who Night* in 1999. Once more, these were seen as workman-like successes – but once again they didn't seem to lead anywhere. And, to make matters worse for David, it was Matt who did the voices in many of the audio versions of *Doctor Who* in the next few years while Christopher Eccleston and David Tennant would subsequently get the plum roles of reviving the television franchise.

It was at this low point that the pair began to feel that the big time was going to pass them by. They felt they had been working too hard, for too long – and had got too little in return. Maybe this was time to call it a day and look for – neither of them liked the phrase – a proper job.

As luck would have it, that decision never had to be made. Because just as they were about to give up hope, they got the news that they had spent nearly five years hoping for. It turned out that someone at the BBC had seen Sir Bernard Chumley's latest act. (In their second and third years in Edinburgh, they had rewritten their original 'And Friends' act and renamed it 'Sir Bernard Chumley Gangshow' with a whole new cast of cameo roles for David. The following year they had taken yet another act, 'Sir Bernard Chumley's Grand Tour', on the road.) Their new fan in Broadcasting House thought that in the right format the all-new Sir Bernard could at last be ready for mainstream television. So he tracked his creators down and told them what he wanted.

'Six episodes – the BBC wants six fucking episodes!' Matt and David simply couldn't believe it. After all this time and so many near misses, they were finally signing a contract that could change their lives.

Both knew – and had both been told in no uncertain terms by BBC2 – that their foul-mouthed live act would not work on terrestrial television. What the channel liked was Sir Bernard's underlying character. Matt and David's task in 1999 was to clean him up and come up with the format and programme structure that would do him justice.

A lot of peppermint tea was drunk in north London as the pair set out to do just that. They went back over all the scenarios they had put him in so far, trying to remember how each had been received by different audiences. And they tried to work out a way to give BBC2 viewers what they might expect – but with a twist. The idea, when it came, was simple. They were going to follow the heritage trail. Sir Bernard would parody Middle England's obsession with country houses and National Trust properties. And with a bit of luck he would raise a lot of eyebrows in the process.

The show that the men came up with was to be called *Sir Bernard's Stately Homes*. Old friends and colleagues Myfanwy Moore, Jon Plowman and Edgar Wright were on board as producer, executive producer and director respectively, and while filming was rushed and stressful everyone had great fun. The idea was to balance Sir Bernard out with some of the best cameo characters from the live act. Most of them were to be played by David, though old faithfuls Paul Putner and David Foxxe were also on the team and Julie T Wallace, Rowland Rivron and even Jools Holland signed up to play some bit parts. Everyone knew that they didn't have much time to make an impact. Each episode was just ten minutes long, so every second had to count. Matt and David's view was that it didn't much matter if the jokes were verbal or visual. They just had to stuff them in and keep them coming.

Episode one kicked off with Sir Bernard conducting a camera crew around Baxter Grange, supposedly the former home of Admiral Nelson (the name of every fictional location in the series had a link to *Grange Hill* – a visual joke they would repeat years later when every tower block in *Little Britain* was named after a character from *Whose Line Is It Anyway?*). Right from the start, the pair wanted Sir Bernard's theatrical bitterness to come to the fore, so they had him appear to go off script, ranting about how Peter Ustinov had once beaten him to the role of Nelson in a big-budget film. Matt's Sir Bernard, of course, was sourness personified about how Sir Peter had performed. 'It wasn't Nelson. I'm sorry, but it wasn't. Ustinov's fine if you want some sort of comedy Chink or an obese French copper, but he just wasn't Horatio. He's not even an actor. He's just an overweight man who tells stories. And his impressions are rubbish.'

David's character Anthony Rogers (a 'misunderstood' wife-murderer on probation) was introduced and the plot raced on. The series would move through Browning Abbey, Yates Castle, Bronson House and Kendall Park to Stebson Towers (the *Grange Hill* references becoming ever more obtuse) and as it did so the plot got ever more complicated and surreal.

There were all the men dressed as women that would characterise Matt and David's later work. And some of the 'word from our sponsors' voice-overs were already pure *Little Britain*. ('Allen's Crisps: At last a crisp for straights and gays alike' being just one example.) The in-jokes for telly addicts came thick and fast and the language and sexual references were about as strong as BBC2 could take.

Matt and David were thrilled with the whole process, however. And by the time they had finished writing the final episode they felt Sir Bernard had been totally reinvigorated and had a huge amount of new mileage in him. 'I can see Sir Bernard spreading his drama gospel throughout the country: trying to excavate the Pomegranate Theatre buried under the Lakeside shopping centre, re-enacting plays in Dixons, or leading drama therapy classes in borstal,' said Matt, his words tripping over each other with enthusiasm as he was asked what might be the follow-up to *Stately Homes*. David, meanwhile, had written out a host of new programme ideas for a possible follow-up and was hoping to present them to the BBC as soon as possible.

So the whole production team was in a fantastic mood at 10.20pm on Wednesday, 12 May 1999, when the first episode of the series was broadcast. Yes, there were rough edges and some slight miscalculations in the timing and the script. But overall, Matt and David thought to themselves as the closing titles ran, it works well and it's only going to get better from here. They had been wrong to have bad feelings about 1999 – this, they were sure, was going to be their best year yet and Sir Bernard was going to push them into the entertainment A-list. They simply couldn't have been more excited about the way things were working out.

Or at least that was how they felt until the critics had their say. The following day, the pair got the sort of bad reviews that could stop a train. Both men felt almost physically sick as they read the commentaries. All publicity is supposed to be good publicity. But this was off the scale and Sir Bernard's latest comic adventure seemed over before it had even begun.

The infamously savage Victor Lewis-Smith in the London *Evening Standard* was first in line with a series of killer blows. 'Theatrical raconteur Sir Bernard Chumley is the creation of Matt Lucas and he is noteworthy for three things: a dreadful rug, an accent that veers between Belgravia and Bermondsey (sometimes intentionally, sometimes not) and a visceral hatred of other, more successful thespians,' was how the review began. 'Last night's tour around "the ancestral home of Lord Nelson" began promisingly enough, although the deliberately crass message from his sponsors ("in association with Allen's crisps, the cheaper crisp") was a little too close to the truth in Lucas's case. Sorry, but it ill-behoves a man whose career to date has peaked with a series of Cadbury's Creme Egg commercials to point the finger at actors who shamelessly exploit their fame for money. "Work started on Baxter Grange in 1805, the house was completed in 1805, and in 1805 Nelson took up residence until his death in 1805," he began, neatly parodying the jumble of unmemorable and unremembered facts with which visitors to stately homes are invariably assaulted by tour guides.

'But oh dear. Just as I was delighting in the fact that Lucas had finally divested himself of partner David Walliams, the dismally untalented man popped up in the role of a jobsworth gardener. Living proof that you are only young once, but you can stay immature indefinitely, he persistently interrupted the filming in the mistaken belief that he possesses the stroppy charm and immaculate comic timing of a Michael Palin (he doesn't).

'From then on, the programme speedily went downmarket,' Lewis-Smith continued, before gearing up for one final savage attack. 'A plot about finding the location of a mysterious "golden potato" hove fleetingly into view late in the day, but such a flimsy premise cannot possibly bear the weight of six episodes and by the end of this first instalment Lucas was already reduced to dressing up as a pirate with a plastic parrot on his shoulder and shouting, "Aaah, Jim lad." Not only was it desperately unfunny, but it was tragically similar to a dire routine that Tony Hancock used to perform in the Galton-and-Simpsonless twilight of his career. But at least he had the decency to commit suicide afterwards. A spoof documentary about stately homes is a potential gold mine for a keen-eyed comic. The hilarious conflict raging within the soul of every aristo who opens his house to the public (hating the rabble, but needing the money) could keep any half-decent writer busy for a lifetime, yet this was unobservant, badly scripted, semi-improvised tosh.'

The Lewis-Smith conclusion offered an equally bleak piece of advice for its stars. 'Having died on our screens last night, why don't they host a television first next week, by offering us a 10-minute silence during their next 10-minute show?' he asked.

'Jesus. Jesus Christ. How can we recover from that?' David in particular was horrified by the venom in many of the early reviews of *Sir Bernard's Stately Homes*. By definition, this was such a public failure. Everyone back on the comedy circuit and the crew of all the one-off and pilot shows they had made in the past few frantic years had been desperately envious of their move on to mainstream television. Now everyone would be expecting them to go back to the bad late-night live slots and the satellite channels, with their tails between their legs. The humiliation was complete. And what made matters worse was the old showbusiness belief that nothing fails quite so successfully as failure. Bad reviews tended to beget more bad reviews – and the nature of television criticism was that after such a drubbing for their first show the men knew they could expect more of the same on most other papers for the rest of the series. They were right, and papers that had ignored the show's first episode fired back with some savagery of their own the following week.

Having been applauded on the comedy circuit, Sir Bernard, it seemed, was almost universally disliked in the mainstream media. 'He is a parody of elder statesman actors and is portrayed as a racist, greedy, pig–ignorant, snobbish bore. And he is the most likeable of all the creations on show,' wrote one online commentator. 'It is a round of satirical stabs delivered completely without affection,' wrote another.

And this was perhaps the hardest thing of all for Matt and David to read – for it confirmed once again the most common threat of criticism that had dogged them since they had first teamed up as writers nearly five years earlier. So had they yet again overstepped the mark and repelled rather than charmed their audience? Were they just too tough, too caustic and too angry to make it in the mainstream? Three years previously, after their Barrymore debacle, they had vowed to try and lighten up their act. Less than 12 months earlier, after the reviews for *Boyz Unlimited*, they had said the same thing. Clearly, on both occasions they had failed to follow through.

Feeling at their lowest ebb, the pair jumped at the chance to get as far as possible from the British critics as the series ended. They had signed up to appear at the 'Just for Laughs' Comedy Festival in Montreal alongside a top-notch British contingent that included Ed Byrne, Dave Gorman, Jeff Green, Richard Morton, Ross Noble, Graham Norton and Johnny Vegas. These were all Matt and David's biggest rivals in the comedy world – the people they most wanted to impress. If Sir Bernard had been better received on television, Matt and David could have seen this overseas tour as a chance to revel in their triumph and settle some informal scores. As it was, they knew that everyone flying over to Canada with them would have read the reviews for *Stately Homes* and would know just how damaged their act had become.

And it should have been so different. When they had signed up for the Canadian gig Matt and David had also hoped it would be a springboard to take Sir Bernard up to the next level of success. That year the festival was primarily a trade show, where the industry searched out new talent from within – it was where careers could be made. What Matt and David needed to know now was whether it was also where they could be rebuilt.

Fortunately, both men had long since learned that if you want to make it as a comedian you need to be thick skinned. You need to be able to shake off all the set-backs and humiliations and carry on with the show. You need to get back on stage and start telling jokes even when no one else is laughing. So as their plane left London they vowed to front it out with their rivals and give Sir Bernard one last try. It was the right decision. But, as bad luck would have it, things started to go wrong from the moment they got on to the Canadian stage.

In Montreal, the British acts were all being filmed for a BBC1 show, a showcase that could have triggered Sir Bernard's television rehab. Or it could have done if Matt's radio mike hadn't failed for almost their entire seven-minute set, leaving half the audience pretty much unable to hear a thing that he said while the rest treated his pre-written anger and toilet humour with barely concealed disdain.

'After the show, Dave and I rerecorded our set to an empty room and the BBC people said they would cue the laughter on afterwards so hopefully it wasn't a complete disaster and no one would ever know,' said Matt.

But both men felt it was yet another sign that Sir Bernard's best days were over. He had taken them to some of the biggest comedy venues at the Edinburgh Festival. He had taken them to clubs and shows around the country. He had taken them overseas and on to national television. But, while his trademark had been to be savage to his audience, those audiences had ended up being even more savage in return.

With their confidence at an all-time low, it seemed as if the magic had finally gone out of their act. And when this happens, as both men knew, you have to move on. They were in silence as they left their hotel and prepared for the journey back to Britain. They had to face the fact that Sir Bernard Chumley, the biggest and most established project of their careers, had been sunk. And this time they knew it was going to be very, very hard to swim away from the wreckage.

CHAPTER 8

SEPARATE WAYS?

Back from Canada and holed up in their respective north London flats, the pair seriously considered going their separate ways – and, in doing so, preventing the world from ever witnessing *Little Britain*. 'I did worry back then that we might have missed our moment, that everyone in television had finally seen us and passed on us,' admitted David, years later, reflecting on how close the duo had come to a professional break-up after Sir Bernard Chumley's big implosion.

As the new millennium approached, Matt had been thinking the same – and he was the first to break free. He had enjoyed the most success so far and could perhaps have done more as a solo comedian. But he still felt bruised from the television critics and from the snarl-ups at the Canadian comedy festival. What he needed was a complete change of pace – and a bit of a break from the spotlight. So far the Lucas/Walliams double act had differed from those of all their comic heroes because Matt had dominated its public face. David had shared all the writing, producing and directing duties and had slogged away behind the scenes writing letters, making phone calls and signing them up for work. But, while his warm-up and cameo roles had always been important to the act, it had always been Matt who had dominated the main event. In 2000, as his eighth anniversary as a stand-up approached, Matt was starting to get tired of always carrying a show. He was also losing a little bit of confidence in his own lines.

With this in mind, the chance to act in a play seemed too good to miss – especially if he could lose himself in the middle of a big cast. Acting also seemed therapeutic after the stresses of the past few years. It was like going back to his best days at Haberdashers' Aske's school when life suddenly seemed to have been a whole lot simpler.

With all this in mind, Matt auditioned for the role of Thersites in the Oxford Stage Company's production of *Troilus and Cressida*. The play, directed by Dominic Dromgoole, had a cast of 21, led by Jordan Murphy as Troilus and Eileen Walsh as Cressida. Both were rapidly rising stars – Jordan had just won a Tony award on Broadway for his role in *The Beauty Queen of Leenane* while Eileen had just stared in her first Britflick film, *Janice Beard 45wpm*. When he was told he had got the job alongside them, Matt felt a huge sense of relief. He knew that for a change the real weight of the show would fall on their shoulders rather than on his. And, as the opening night approached in the spring of 2000, that was just what he needed.

The other reason that he took on such a small-scale role was less easy to admit to, however. It was because very few other doors had been open to him at that point – and he was terrified of being out of work. 'I had a taste of how the business works with *Shooting Stars*,' he told a journalist who sat in on some of the early *Troilus and Cressida* rehearsals. 'I know what it is like to be touring in front of 3,000 people a night every week and having people all wearing your T-shirt. And I know what it is like three years later when none of this is happening any more. The career of a comic is not an upward trajectory. You peak and then you go down. So why am I doing this play? Why not? I'm as likely to do a straight play as more comedy,' he said, with an unusual flatness in his voice.

Of course, having long since accepted that his appearance meant he was unlikely to ever be cast as a serious leading man, Matt did still try and inject as much humour as possible into his new role. The play itself, while poorly known, is in fact described as 'Shakespeare's most shockingly modern play and a comic masterpiece of rage and filth'. So it seemed to fit Matt like a glove from day one. His character (which, coincidentally, had once been played by Ken Dodd) was that of the bitter clown who commentates on the battles between the Greeks and the Trojans. And Matt grabbed as much licence with the role as he could. 'Matt Lucas plays Thersites in the style of strange Jewish vaudeville, as much *Underneath the Arches* as Beckett tramp, with snatches of modern songs, almost inaudibly hummed, old-fashioned nods to the audience and a natural comic's attempt to inject pace into the void of the production,' wrote one critic.

Others were not as convinced, however. Many reviewers hated the whole production – and said Matt was just dragging it even further down. 'One begins to look forward to the appearance of Matt Lucas's Thersites. Not because he acts well – he doesn't – but because his improvised interjections have more energy than anything else in this plodding, confused production,' wrote one London paper bitingly.

The show was being performed at the Old Vic in London and on tour around the country – and, if nothing else, Matt says it was good for his stamina. The cast did eight three-hour performances a week, and had to stay behind and take part in Q&A sessions with the audience after most of them.

For all the mixed reactions from the critics, by the time the end of the run came, Matt was convinced that he had been right to take on the role. The camaraderie of being in a big travelling cast had helped him out of his post-Sir Bernard depression. It had rekindled his love of live theatre and reaffirmed his desire to one day write a West End musical. It had also earned him one of his favourite, if least comprehensible, reviews.

'Lucas manages to suggest that Thersites's reductive vision of the Trojan war as an argument over a whore and a cuckold contains an implied moral positive,' it said. I did? Matt asked himself on reading it. I thought I was just acting in a play. And anyway, was his implied moral

Above: Matt as part of Fat Les for the unofficial World Cup song *Vindaloo*. From left: artist Damien Hirst, Keith Allen and Alex James of Blur far right.

Below: With *Shooting Stars* co-stars Vic Reeves and Bob Mortimer. Matt's turn as George Dawes on the show was a big hit, and Bob was to be something of a mentor to him during his early struggles to make it in the industry.

Above: Matt and David, here hamming it up as Simon and Garfunkel, with presenter Jamie Theakston on *Rock Profile*. The show was the first real television success for the pair.

Below left: The pair with comedian Steve Coogan, with whom David co-starred in *Cruise of the Gods*.

Below right: David with comedian and friend Rob Brydon, who also starred in *Cruise of the Gods*. Rob and David were planning to make a sitcom together until the success of *Little Britain*, and Rob later worked as a script editor on the show.

Above: Matt at the launch of Boy George's musical *Taboo* in which he starred. The show received mixed reviews.

Below left: David with Ralf Little. The pair rolled out more of their *Rock Profile* characters for the last time on *The Ralf Little Show*, before they began work on *Little Britain*.

Below right: Former Doctor Who star Tom Baker, who did the voice overs for *Little Britain*, was seen as being vital to the success of the show.

'Yeah but no but…' Matt Lucas as Vicky Pollard.

Above: *Buffy the Vampire* star Anythony Head, who played the role of Prime Minister in *Little Britain*. The boys considered it something of a coup to land such an established star, and his presence gave the recording sessions a real lift.

Below: David Walliams playing Sebastian, the PM's lovelorn aide.

Above left: Fat fighters group leader Marjorie Dawes.

Above right: As Andy and Lou, voted as the stars of the most popular *Little Britain* sketch

Below: 'We're Lay-dees!' Matt as Florence and David as Emily.

The only gay in the village: Matt as Daffyd Thomas.

David with his award for Best Newcomer at the 2003 British Comedy Awards – the first of many awards the show was to garner its stars with.

positive a good thing or a bad one? Should he try and do that more, or less, in future performances? And what the hell is a 'reductive vision' anyway? To this day, no one involved in the production is entirely sure.

While Matt was making new friends in the theatrical world, an equally dejected David was throwing himself in front of his own new range of challenges. For a while, he too wanted to take a break from the brutality of the live stand-up circuit. But he was convinced he still had what it took to write for other comedians and sitcoms. So he got back on the phone, spoke to some former contacts and rejoined the 'behind-the-scenes' world of comedy creation. Contributing a joke here and a sketch there was the usual hand-to-mouth existence that both Matt and David had lived for so many years while juggling all their other projects. But David was also looking for a new direction outside of the comedy and the stand-up world – and his search was about to strike gold with a straight role in a flagship BBC drama called *Attachments*.

Despite admitting he didn't even know how to use Teletext, let alone the internet, David made it through three rounds of auditions and several improvisation exercises before being given the job (though he says he nearly failed at those because his urge to treat everything as a comedy sketch meant his early auditions weren't quite as serious as the producers had been expecting). The cast filmed for nearly four months in the Old Street area of East London and in Acton, on the other side of town. It was a big-budget show with a vast production team and a lot of unusual added extras. For a start, a fictional interactive website had been set up to run alongside the show and mirror the site that viewers would see being set up on screen – and a host of other dot-com elements were promised as the series got going. 'Aspects of this show are like nothing that has ever been seen before on British television and it is bursting with energy and drive,' said BBC Controller Jane Root at the show's high-profile launch. The series certainly had a good pedigree, as it had been created by many of the same people behind the hit *This Life* and was being shown when everything from Lastminute.com to Amazon had made the internet the biggest talking point in the country.

David was certainly in tune with his character – the slick and sexually ambiguous clothes horse Jake Plasgow whose bisexual girlfriend persuaded him to take part in a threesome with one of their colleagues. 'We all had to sign nudity clauses before we did the series and I kept thinking, Oh, God, when is my turn going to come?' he said of the full-frontal scenes that characterised the series. 'And I would also warn every actor not to think they will be safe just because their contracts say nudity will be filmed on a closed set. All that means is that the person holding the towel will look away.'

Despite several shots of David's naked buttocks (which can still be seen on several internet sites today), viewing figures were disappointing. And while David, like most of his fellow cast members, had signed up to be available for up to three series, the show was soon in trouble. The 50-minute episodes of the second series were cut to just 30 and the third series was never filmed.

The experience had been worthwhile, however, not least for letting casting agents (and several million viewers) know that a new tall, dark and handsome actor was in the market for some work. This ultimately led to a role in an equally ill-fated ITV show, *High Stakes*, though on a more positive note David says he learned a huge amount from the show's star, Richard Wilson. Being with so many good actors on both shows rekindled some of David's earliest ambitions – at exactly the same time that *Troilus and Cressida* was doing the same for Matt. 'When I was young, all my early heroes were actors,' David says. 'I had always wanted to be an actor and at the very beginning I had seen comedy as a good way into the profession. I stayed because I fell in love with comedy, but it had never been my main goal to tell jokes.' Being in a straight drama like *Attachments* also forced David to refine his acting skills. 'Comedy is acting, but it is a far more external process and you can let a lot of external features and props do some of the work for you. Pure acting is far more internal and I found I had to keep reminding myself of this on *Attachments*. I kept looking for the comedy in the scenes and kept forgetting that this wasn't always appropriate.'

David says he also had to get used to the strange experience of seeing his own face looking back at him from the mirror when he left make-up. 'Normally I like looking in the mirror and seeing someone different. Here I look in the mirror and see myself, which sometimes seems to add to the pressure of your performance.'

When the *Attachments* cast and crew were told that the final series had definitely been shelved, a reinvigorated David was ready to move on to other opportunities. He was writing furiously for David Baddiel, as well as for Vic and Bob's new show *Randall & Hopkirk (Deceased)* and a host of his favourite sci-fi shows. The following year, David also won a role in a big-budget comedy drama, *Cruise of the Gods*, as the third man in a cast headed by Steve Coogan and Rob Brydon – a team that were on their way to becoming good friends. The storyline was typically bizarre, with plenty of in-jokes about the nature of showbusiness, fame and television. In a nutshell, the former stars of a fictional sci-fi drama called *Children of Castor* were reunited for a convention of hard-core fans on a cruise ship. What made the story work was the fact that the lives of the show's original stars could hardly have gone in more different directions since filming had stopped. Brydon's character had fallen on hard times and he had quit acting and was working as a hotel porter when the cruise was launched. Coogan's character, however, had gone on to hit the jackpot in America as the star of an improbable blockbuster show called *Sherlock Holmes in Miami*. David, meanwhile, simply camped it up as the obsessed fan Jeff 'Lurky' Monks.

Finally shown over Christmas 2002, the show got a mixed reception. Coogan and Brydon were both nominated for acting awards and the show itself won a couple of cult television honours. But many hard-core comedy fans slammed it – having expected a pure romp rather than the darker comedy drama that was on offer. For David, it had been another great experience, however. How bad, after all, could a long shoot in the Mediterranean be, he asked. (Pretty bad, actually, after their ship ran aground near Athens and they were forced to finish the work on a replica in the slightly less glamorous Shepperton Studios in Middlesex.)

By the time *Cruise of the Gods* had finished filming, let alone before it had been shown, David had been doing some serious thinking about his future. His foray back into acting had been useful in a host of different ways – not least by paying quite a few of the bills that Sir Bernard Chumley had never been able to cover. But, for all his original love of great actors, David felt the pull back to pure, unashamed comedy. 'I suddenly realised that deep down it is a lot more fun doing comedy. You're making people laugh, after all. And I think my future is still going to be in that area,' he said when he and Matt first started working on separate projects. When those other projects had run their course he decided to give comedy another go. And he knew straight away that there was nobody he wanted to share that world with more than Matt.

Fortunately, Matt was thinking the same. Slogging his way through Shakespeare at the Old Vic and contributing the odd gag or sketch to Ali G, Lenny Beige, Dennis Pennis and the writing teams behind *The League of Gentlemen* in his time off, Matt was itching to find a new project. He and David got back into their old habits of whiling away a few hours in a West Hampstead café talking about popular culture and jotting down notes about ways to spoof or parody it. They started loafing around at home, bouncing ideas around. They also returned to their tried-and-tested formula of watching every piece of junk television that they could find. And that summer it turned out that there was plenty to choose from.

The biggest show, and the hardest to ignore, was *Big Brother*. The second series had just begun and the country was being introduced to a new set of housemates led by Welsh hairdresser Helen 'I like blinking, I do' Adams, whose relationship with computer designer Paul Clarke seemed to be fascinating the whole country.

But, from their sofas, Matt and David both found themselves becoming increasingly interested in another big dynamic within the group. It was the year that show host Davina McCall revealed that the *Big Brother* producers had tricks up their sleeves – and one of those tricks was to introduce an extra character into the series in the third week to try and jolt the existing housemates out of their early equilibrium. That new housemate was the handsome gay businessman Josh Rafter. Everyone in the house got a shock when the 32-year-old walked through the doors and into the compound – with 22-year-old Ryanair steward Brian Dowling affected most of all.

Millions of *Big Brother* viewers had spent the past two weeks watching how Brian, a man who had previously only come out to his parents, had started to revel in the new sense of freedom he found in the house. He mentioned his gayness on a daily if not hourly basis, seemingly convinced that it gave him an edge, a mystique and a status that he might not otherwise have had in the company of so many other strong personalities. As his initial shyness faded away, his antics became even more outrageous. Or at least they did until Josh arrived.

'As far as Brian was concerned, the gay thing was definitely his thing and no one else was having it,' says Matt.

'When Josh came into the house, not only was Brian's identity threatened but also the idea of being around a gay man who was obviously quite sexual was incredibly threatening to him,' David adds.

The dynamic meant even more to Matt and David than just another good reality-television moment, because they had already sketched out a very similar comedy character. Their creation, based on a mutual friend who had wrongly felt his coming out would cause the world to stop, was still half-formed. Brian helped them put it all together. 'When we saw Brian, we knew our character, Daffyd, had a truth to him. Brian was basically acting out the whole thing for us and it was brilliant to watch it all being played out for real,' says Matt.

Turning off the television one night after Brian and Josh had survived yet another eviction vote, Matt and David felt a fresh wave of creativity. The one thing that had always driven them – their ability to create closely observed and inherently comic characters – had seemed to disappear with Sir Bernard Chumley. Now it was back. And once again all they needed was a proper arena in which to display them.

But were they really ready to find a framework for the embryonic Daffyd and all the other new ideas buzzing around in their brains? For a while, they agreed that they weren't – because another cultural trend had attracted their professional attention. The cult of the pop star celebrity was gaining ever more currency, largely propelled by the open-audition talent shows like *Pop Stars: The Rivals*. The way these new celebrities spoke, acted, behaved and justified their newfound fame seemed ripe for a fresh type of parody – the type of parody that Matt and David reckoned they could do better than anyone. They went back over all the notes they had made while devising *Boyz Unlimited*. As they did so, they saw how the profiles of the more established pop stars seemed to rise alongside those of the reality-show winners – with the inconsequential opinions of even the most vapid performers seeming to carry more weight than those of politicians or even the prime minister.

As the men pondered the phenomenon, they took a call from old friend Myfanwy Moore. She asked if they wanted to film a few of the 'blink-and-you-miss-them' *Funny Noise* slots that introduced the videos on the BBC's fledgling Play UK channel. Harry Enfield, Simon Pegg and a group of other comedians had done a couple and there was some money left in the budget for a few more. *Funny Noise* was about as basic as you could get. You stood in front of a single camera and performed about a minute of material. The odds were that no one important would ever see them – but at this point neither Matt nor David felt in a position to turn down work, however humble. Their contributions were brief but often characteristically surreal. They portrayed Brian May and Anita Dobson as a two-headed, twin-wigged monster. They recreated Björk as the ventriloquist dummy on Keith Harris's knee. And they shot a quick scene as The Bee Gees in which Barry Gibb had a tail and a lion's whiskers.

It was this final idea that really got the pair thinking – because they were certain that there was more mileage in it. The more they researched the subject, the more they thought that all the new superstars of the music scene were ripe for a proper parody. As usual, all they needed was the platform. And as it happened they were about to be offered it. *Funny Noise* had got them noticed – and *Rock Profile* was about to be born.

CHAPTER 9

ROCK PROFILE

'I'm not doing it. I'm not doing it. I'm not doing it. Who put those flowers there?'

'You did.'

'I don't care. I'm still not doing it. I hate interviews. I loathe them. And that Jamie Theakston's an abomination.'

It was hardly a new idea to portray Elton John as an over-the-top and endlessly demanding drama queen — it was an image that had been set in stone after the 1996 fly-on-the-wall documentary *Tantrums and Tiaras* made by his partner David Furnish. But the sheer pace that Matt and David gave to their parody in *Rock Profile* set it above all their competitors — and it explains why Elton himself says it is his all-time favourite spoof.

Rock Profile had been commissioned as a natural progression of *Funny Noise* — and at the time it didn't look as if it was much of a step forward for its creators. The good news was that the films were longer — around ten minutes each. But they were still only designed to be fillers between Play UK's videos, just as Matt and David's sitcom spoofs had been used as fillers for Channel Four's sitcom night what felt like a lifetime ago. At first the men were convinced that their work would once more get swallowed up by the shows alongside it and disappear without trace. And in the late 1990s it was true that Play UK was hardly the place to get noticed. At several points in the day it tended to have so few viewers that it fell off the ratings charts altogether. And the tiny number of music lovers who did watch the channel were switching on to see the latest Robbie Williams, Backstreet Boys or Texas video – not the low-budget programmes that were shown around them.

Or at least that was what happened until *Rock Profile* came along. Unlike any of the work the pair had done before, this got a genuine buzz from the start. People started talking about the spoofs – described as 'mini rockumentaries'. They were repeated on a near-constant loop and after a while viewers began to prefer them to the main events they were scheduled around. At one point, Play UK even started beating some rival stations in the audience satisfaction surveys and, while viewing figures were still low, a secondary market in taped copies of the spoofs earned them a far bigger audience. For the first time in their careers, Matt and David were on a real roll. This is what momentum feels like, they said to themselves. They didn't know where it might take them. But they liked it.

Writing and filming the *Rock Profile* shows was hard

work, but great fun. The men say that from the start they were determined to go beyond just replicating a traditional impression show. 'After we had been broadcasting for a while someone called our work "unimpressions", which may well have been designed to insult us, but it was actually a very good description. That was pretty much what we were aiming to achieve. Our idea was to develop characters rather than do impressions,' says Matt.

'A good impression is something you only want to see for about 30 seconds,' was David's theory. 'It would be pointless, for example, to see someone do an impression of, say, Ronnie Corbett, for 15 minutes. But you could watch a sketch like that for 15 minutes if it was subtly picking up all the things we think or imagine about Ronnie Corbett and presenting them in a way no one had quite thought of before.'

The pair's starting point was to decide on celebrities to study (they tended to put two singers together so they both had a role to play). Then they drew up a list of the person's real and imagined characteristics – the things that made them famous, the gossip everyone had heard about them, the subjects they tend to talk about most frequently in interviews and those that they tend to shy away from. It was, they say, like putting together a jigsaw, with dozens of pieces slowly fitting together into an entirely new picture. Having looked at each individual 'victim', they then sat down to work out how the two they were going to portray together might interact. Were they really as good friends as they said they were? Was there something odd about their body language in photographs or past interviews that could be picked up on and exaggerated out of all proportion? Was there something else that could be imagined about them? A rivalry? A secret passion? A terrible secret in their past? Poring over their notes and rereading an endless number of past interviews, Matt and David let their imaginations run wild.

But, throughout this whole process, they also tried to keep one important thought at the forefront of their minds. Both were well aware that much of their previous work had been attacked as too tough, too uncompromising, too cruel. They were determined not to make the same mistakes again. 'We had to be a bit mean in some of the *Rock Profile* portrayals to make them funny, but we are certainly not trying to undermine any of the people we feature. There is real affection in all of them and we hope this shines through,' Matt said at the time.

Perhaps strangely, the very last part of the pre-production job was deciding which role the two creators would play. Sometimes it was obvious – David did look a lot more like, say, David Furnish, George Michael or Bono than Matt. But, as direct impressions were never the main aim, this wasn't as important as viewers might think. Accents were another fluid area. Both men loved the different regional accents that cropped up out of context on shows like *Eurotrash* and *Creature Comforts*. So sometimes it seemed funniest to play a character's accent completely against type as well (David's middle-class, home-counties version of Bono – 'I'm not Irish. I'm from Windsor. I put the accent on for the American market' – was a fantastic example). 'What I loved about writing the scripts was trying to get into the character's head and working out what they might say or how they might react to the situations we have put them in, and given the exaggerated characteristics we have come up with for them,' says David.

But would the show have worked as a series of simple, if off-the-wall, sketches? Matt and David felt that it wouldn't, and that they needed a stronger structure to hold it all together. That was when the interview approach was born. One of the things that they both loved most about modern celebrities was how they could subconsciously give such a lot away about their states of mind in even the softest of interviews. And, of course, how much nonsense they could come up with. Having decided that a similar format would work for them, they scouted around for the perfect host – and found him in the form of fellow National Youth Theatre graduate Jamie Theakston. One year older than David, he was one of the BBC's biggest kids' show presenters, having hosted everything from *Live & Kicking* and *The O-Zone* to *Top of the Pops*. As such, he was immediately associated with the kind of pop stars Matt and David wanted to spoof, so he made the perfect straight man and comic foil.

'The show needed the edge of reality that Jamie provided to make it work and set it apart from other simpler spoofs,' said David. 'He was brilliant, never fluffed his lines and had this perfect bemused look which we could cut to whenever his guest had acted particularly badly.'

Most importantly, Jamie also had a similar sense of humour to his new employers. He was prepared to do the show for almost nothing (of which more later) and was more than happy to send himself up if it raised an extra laugh. His much-publicised visit to a Mayfair brothel over Christmas in 2001 was just one example – the tabloid headlines about his 'three-in-a-bed' visit were, of course, the ones that Steps interviewees H and Lee decided to sing about in a Beatles-style 'I read the news today, oh boy' episode.

As part of a video-based chart channel, Matt and David also had free and easy access to a lot of performance footage to use alongside their early spoofs, footage that had to be removed for copyright reasons when they were reshown on BBC2 and released on DVD. So in that first Elton John and David Furnish show they punctuated the interview with clips from Elton's videos and a stream of 'Rock Facts' captions that were worthy of *Viz* magazine. 'Elton John's marriage to wife Renata failed when he remembered he was gay,' was one of them. Another, a reference to the period in the 1970s and 1980s when the sex, drugs and rock 'n' roll were taking their toll on Elton, read, 'It was awful. I didn't enjoy a single minute of it. That's why I only did it for about 25 years.'

The Elton spoof had begun with a quick pre-interview

section in which David, playing a black-clad, sinister and controlling David Furnish, primly checked that every one of Elton's exacting rock-star whims had been catered for. These included five bowls of fruit in varying stages of ripeness and, for some strange reason, a fun-sized Milky Way at room temperature. When Matt stormed in dressed as Elton in a fuchsia suit, the demands continued. 'Where's my gift?' he demanded, before being presented with a white puppy.

'Oh, I love it. I'll call it doggy. I love it. Right, put it in the bin,' he ordered Furnish, as his attention span reached its end and he moved on to a fresh set of ridiculous requests.

Also under the microscope in that first show was a clever mickey take of the legendary speed with which Elton can apparently put words to music. To prove it, Matt's bejewelled and bewigged character sat at the piano and dashed off a pretty decent song to a fax from lyricist Bernie Taupin that said, 'Sorry I didn't manage to get any lyrics to you today, I'll see what I can do tomorrow. PS my video is on the blink can you tape *Lovejoy* for me.' 'The man's a genius,' said Matt's Elton.

As the series progressed, it was clear that many of Matt and David's other portrayals were uncannily accurate. 'Once or twice, I interviewed the real stars within a day or so of doing the *Rock Profile*. And I have to say Matt and David can be scarily like the real thing,' said Jamie, who said the favourite part of his day on set was waiting to see Matt and David come out of make-up and wardrobe and turn on their characters. It was a moment Jamie actually got to enjoy with increasing frequency – because a minuscule budget meant the *Rock Profile* shooting schedule was fast and furious. A single episode of a soap like *Coronation Street* can have a budget of up to £1 million, while even the cheapest reality shows can cost up to £350,000 an hour to film. Matt and David, however, were spending less than £2,000 an episode on *Rock Profile* – and that included everyone's wages. The sketches were also filmed at breakneck speed. One fully costumed episode was often filmed and finished in the morning with a completely different one shot in the afternoon. 'Everything was incredibly cheaply done and often we all made do with sandwiches from the local garage at lunchtime,' admits Matt. 'It certainly didn't feel like a big-time television show.'

The workers, however, loved it. Old faithful Myfanwy Moore was again on board as executive producer, while Lisa Cavalli-Green, another long-term co-worker, was on hand for the make-up and styling. Pat Farmer, who had created Matt's romper suit for *Shooting Stars*, signed up to do the costumes while actors Steve Furst, Ted Robbins and Paul Putner were ready to work for next to nothing when actors were required to play extra parts. Back at the start, the whole process had felt like a labour of love. But everyone believed in it.

The original brief from Play UK was for 13 episodes and a second series produced a further 13. So over the course of two years almost anyone who was anyone in the pop world faced the chance of being parodied by Lucas and Walliams. The victims ranged from old-timers such as Shirley Bassey and Tom Jones to newer stars such as Kylie and Dannii Minogue. Each had been forensically researched by Matt and David. So the humour began the moment the camera started to roll.

Almost all the programme's many highlights included the spoofs, where the pair had decided to play characters entirely against type. So as well as Bono's soft home-counties accent they also pitched the famously political figure as a money-grabbing control freak who was disinterested in charity, unaware of the famine in Ethiopia and fuming at the 'meanness' of Bob Geldof.

'Meanness? In what way?' asked the deadpan Jamie.

'I never received a penny for Band Aid, even though it was Number One for weeks,' replied David's Bono. 'Come to think of it, we've still not been paid for doing Live Aid.'

Other stars whose personalities had been turned upside down included Bez from Happy Mondays, who was recreated as a jazz dancer desperate to break into West End musicals, while Andrew Ridgeley struggles to cope with the fact that Wham! (and indeed the 1980s) were over. Years ahead of their time, Matt and David also predicted the 'mockney' phenomenon of public-school boys like Guy Ritchie wanting the credibility of coming from the East End – their Damon 'I'm definitely working class because I'm a cockney, ain't I?' Albarn being just one classic example.

As well as his Andrew Ridgeley double act, George Michael was due to get a second *Rock Profile* pairing. Matt and David had decided to follow up the latest celebrity gossip and put him alongside Geri Halliwell. Matt got the Geri gig, and played her as a fantastically self-obsessed and lonely stalker. 'It's funny, I'm always asking men out and they often say they're gay,' she mused, having said she had spent the past five days outside George's home because she knew he was in there. 'I love the gays. I mean, don't get me wrong if I had kids I wouldn't let them anywhere near them. But I love the gays,' she went on as the spoof George Michael squirmed next to her, all black clothes and immaculately clipped goatee.

Other characterisations had also been born out of recent events. Like millions of others, Matt and David had watched in disbelief as Barry Gibb ripped off his microphone and led his two brothers off the set of Clive Anderson's talk show when the host made a joke about the name of their first band (it was Les Tosseurs to which Clive, of course, offered, 'Don't worry. You'll always be tossers to me'). From then it was an easy if inspired step from their first *Funny Noise* idea to the final Lucas/Walliams incarnation of a bullying, controlling lion who sends his brothers to their rooms and only lets them speak when they had his permission. 'When Mother went out, she always left me in charge. We have a system. I'm the older brother by ten months and Mother left me in charge,' he explained.

Michael Jackson and reported best friend Elizabeth Taylor were another obvious set of *Rock Profile* targets – though less obvious was the motivation for Matt's brilliantly bulky Elizabeth Taylor being transformed into a finger-jabbing *EastEnders*-style villain whose accent could strip paint.

Superb costumes were a feature of the whole series – all credit here to Cavalli-Green, who was working on a tiny budget. But not all of them worked as well as originally hoped. Ever wonder why Matt's Shirley Bassey spent her whole sketch reclining on a bed? It wasn't just to show her languid, sybaritic lifestyle. It was mainly because the only dress Matt could get for the role was so tight that he thought he would burst through it in a sensitive area and be arrested for indecent exposure if he stood up. Shirley had been paired up with fellow Welsh singer Tom Jones – and as usual Matt and David thought it would work well if they weren't exactly bosom buddies. Constantly trying to upstage each other over the number of film themes they had each sung, a superbly out-of-touch Shirley starts off by dismissing Tom's involvement with *The Full Monty*. 'It's pure fantasy, absolute nonsense. People aren't unemployed and there is no such thing as Sheffield. And anyway you don't even get to see their cocks at the end,' was her verdict.

An endless series of rival singers are next in line for a curt dismissal. 'Tina Turner? I love her to bits, darling, but she doesn't have the range. Gladys Knight? Doesn't have the range. Bruce Hornsby? Doesn't have the range.'

David's Tom Jones, meanwhile, is played as a kindly but unaccountably simple soul who has worked out a way to earn some extra cash. Yes, women still throw their underwear at him at concerts, he admits. 'I collect them all at the end of a show. If they're from M&S I can take them back, exchange them for a nice sweater or something. They know me there. I get vouchers as well.'

The women from Abba are also depicted as at daggers drawn, with Matt having trowelled on the blue eye shadow as Agnetha. For the Eurythmics spoof, Matt plays Dave Stewart as an evil scientist from Transylvania who created Annie Lennox out of spare body parts stolen from a graveyard. Then there was Matt's Prince as a drunken Scottish busker with David playing his social worker. The list of great characters could go on and on, but final mentions should probably go first to the pairing that Matt and David thought didn't quite work, and then to the one they liked the most.

The former were Kylie and Dannii Minogue. The set-up and the script were typically strong. David's Kylie was the queen bee who mistook her sister for room service and personified the concept of sibling rivalry. What let the pairing down, in David's mind, was something no one could really control. 'At the end of the day I was a six-foot-plus, hairy, flabby man, pretending to be a beautiful pop pixie. It didn't quite work,' he says.

What he and Matt thought worked best of all was their pairing of Take That's Gary Barlow and Howard Donald. Matt was a chubby ball of angry bitterness as Gary – yet another control freak still raging over the break-up of the group and desperate for a second chance at fame. Howard, by contrast, was the village idiot, always trying to please and constantly being bullied by his former lead singer (in one sketch he sleeps under the stairs in Gary's terraced house; in another they are reduced to living in a single room at the Coventry YMCA). As usual, it is the little things that keep the characterisations alive. 'Gary, there's all these empty Quavers packets behind the radiator,' Howard points out in the YMCA before being silenced. 'Robbie Williams ruins it and leaves. Career over, end of game,' Gary yells, reading a fictional 'Chance' card while playing a makeshift 'Take That: The Board Game'.

'Even though Take That are becoming a distant memory, we just love playing those characters,' said David just after the first series had finished. 'Matt loves being Gary and I love Howard. When we get into those roles the ideas just keep on flowing so we want to keep on doing it whatever anyone else thinks.' Amazingly enough, the characters proved to be more enduring than even David would have imagined back at the turn of the millennium. Five years later, at the 2005 Brit Awards, he and Matt pulled on the costumes once more before heading on stage to hand the Brits 25 Best Song Award to an unsuspecting Robbie Williams. In 2006, with Take That back on tour, the opportunities for playing the roles even more were getting even more widespread. Despite their shoestring budgets and fast-forward shooting schedules, the men had managed to create a classic.

For all the fun everyone had making the first set of *Rock Profile* shows, the big issue for Matt and David in 2000 was whether the productions would give them their long-overdue leg up the career ladder. Buried on Play UK, that seemed unlikely. But as usual there was always the hope that a mainstream channel might commission another series, or at least buy up the rights to the first and give them a wider showing. If so, and if the critics are kind, then the sky could be the limit. Matt and David knew they were playing a waiting game – and that if they didn't get somewhere soon it would be too late.

'*Rock Profile* has been great. We've loved doing it, we're very fond of it, very proud of it and very grateful that people like it,' said David after the first series was shown. 'But we look around at our peers and we look at the slots and at the budgets that they get and we do wonder if we have fallen behind and missed our moment. We just think, Oh, what could we do if we got a half-hour comedy slot on BBC2 with the production budget that would entail. We're convinced we have more to offer if we only get the chance.'

What happened in 2000 would go some way towards making the pair's dreams come true, however. Play UK asked for a second series – giving the pair the chance to bring their show count up to 26. And BBC2 then bought the rights to show them all on terrestrial television. The money was still pretty low. But the platform was high. Once again the pair had the unusual sense of feeling a stiff wind behind them. They were being moved in the right direction for a change.

It was October 2001, nearly two years after the first low-budget shows had been filmed, that *Rock Profile* was first shown on BBC2. And it was given a huge amount of support. A big feature article in the *Radio Times* and follow-ups in several national papers and magazines heralded the start of the series. A great word-of-mouth campaign from former Play UK viewers looked set to ensure ratings were strong. So Matt and David knew a hell of a lot would depend on the television critics – people who had rarely cut them much slack in the past.

As bad luck would have it, one of the first people to review the show was Victor Lewis-Smith, in the London *Evening Standard*. He was the man whose brutal criticism had all but destroyed the pair's careers less than two years earlier when he had implied *Sir Bernard Chumley's Stately Homes* was so bad that its creators should consider committing suicide as a favour to their viewers.

When they saw his by-line picture at the top of the review the day after the BBC2 launch programme, neither Matt nor David felt strong enough to read it. But friends soon told them they had to – because Lewis-Smith had turned into their biggest fan. He was giving them the kind of boost they had only ever dreamed of. 'Having spent years slagging off the lamentable comedic efforts of Matt Lucas and David Walliams, I'd like to think that they finally took notice of my constructive criticism and decided to raise their game,' he began. 'But, in reality, I bet they completely ignored me (like every other sodding performer I've written about during the past 147 years) and simply floundered about until (either by luck or judgement) they finally found a format that suited them.' The format in question, he explained, was *Rock Profile*.

'It is getting a deserved terrestrial screening on BBC2 and I've watched the entire series and every programme sparkles – particularly the Bee Gees with Barry Gibb portrayed as a lion,' Lewis-Smith concluded.

Holding on to the paper in north London, Matt and David could hardly believe it. Their nemesis had turned into their biggest supporter. And, just as Lewis-Smith's first bad review had triggered a raft of similar bile from other critics two years ago, so his positive opinions brought forward similar praise from rival reviewers this time around. Suddenly Matt and David really started to feel as if they were on their way.

What made things even better was the fact that the stars they were parodying every week were equally happy to admit how great they found the shows. George Michael said he became a huge Lucas/Walliams fan after watching *Rock Profile*. (He and Geri would often ring each other after each show to laugh about it. Years later, he was still such a big fan of the comedians that he cut short a play-through of his new album because he wanted to be home in time to watch *Little Britain* live rather than taping it.)

Geri herself apparently took a while to get into the pair's sense of humour, but she did ultimately become a fan as well. 'When Geri met David at a party recently, she spent the whole night quoting me, quoting her,' Matt said. 'I don't eat nothing yellow!' being her favourite, off-the-wall phrase.

Robbie Williams would also quote 'his' sketches to friends endlessly – and he repeated them word-perfect to Matt and David whenever they met up at industry events. 'Not surprisingly he seemed to like the Gary Barlow and Howard Donald one best of all, probably because it showed Gary Barlow in such a terrible light,' admitted David later.

Robbie, George and Elton would give the strongest indication of their support for the spoofs four years later when they each appeared alongside Matt and David in Comic Relief sketches. This kind of long-term celebrity endorsement proved that the pair had been right to move on from their traditional 'take no prisoners' style of aggressive, unpleasant characterisations. Giving up on the old hatchet jobs had been a wise move – though a few famous faces still failed to see the funny side of the show.

Boy George, who would have other fallings out with Matt in the future when the latter took a lead role in his musical *Taboo*, was one of the few to be unimpressed by his *Rock Profile*. 'I saw your show,' was all he said to Matt when they passed each other at a work function shortly after broadcast. Just four words, then he turned away.

The final challenge of *Rock Profile* was whether or not it could stand a few big set-piece shows as well as the standard interview formats. It passed the first test when

Matt and David decided to lampoon the recording of a new Blur single. Some of the riffs and the chords were perfectly in tune with the band's style. The lyrics, however, were as appalling as Matt and David could make them, which led to the final joke of the performance.

'What do you think? It's got No 1 written all over it,' says Matt as Damon Albarn after the final notes of the recording have faded.

'No, I think it's got more of a whiff of No 2,' says Jamie, with a trademark glance at the camera as the credits rolled.

As proof that they were finally making career headway, a third series of *Rock Profile* was commissioned – and the men decided to take a gamble. Instead of filming another dozen interviews, they would make a single 45-minute show based on the recording of a spoof charity single. It was an ambitious idea, requiring a strong narrative thread and a host of cameo appearances dressed up as more than 15 of their favourite artists. Top of the list was Gary Barlow, and the whole show was built around the idea of him using the charity angle as a way to revive his career. The next big joke was the choice of the charity and the song – the show was called *Rock the Blind* and Gary had picked the hideously inappropriate 'I Can See Clearly Now' for the fundraiser, with Stevie Wonder jetting in to sing the chorus.

The show ended with a deliberately clichéd video (using the backdrop to Lou Reed's 'Perfect Day') and in the editing suite everyone agreed it was a strong package. The budget had been far higher than on either of the

previous two *Rock Profile* series, and it showed. Jamie
Theakston, who popped up throughout the 45 minutes
alongside some other real-life interviewers, was
particularly convinced they had filmed a winner. But
then things went wrong. UK Play was suddenly under
new management – and the latest bosses were not keen
on any of the shows that the previous incumbents had
commissioned. *Rock the Blind*, therefore, was buried in the
schedules and hardly ever repeated. It got a fraction of the
audience of the two series of *Rock Profile* and pretty much
disappeared without trace.

For Matt and David, it was yet another bitter
disappointment after a huge amount of effort. But still
the work went on. If *Rock the Blind* didn't work, then
maybe something else would. They got their *Rock Profile*
characters back on the road, filming segments for as many
other shows as possible – *The Priory, Top of the Pops* and
even a licence fee advert for the BBC in the hope that
this would get the top brass interested in them. They
carried on making lists of new stars to spoof – David was
determined to play Anastasia, for example, while they
built up a sketch of Madonna as a single mother with a
rough Brummie accent.

The other big job that came up in this fallow period
was on BBC3's *The Ralf Little Show*. As well as making a
rare guest appearance as themselves, Matt and David also
filmed a new set of pop spoofs as inserts. Charlotte
Church, Will Young and Gareth Gates were the three
most popular new characters with the audience, but two

other creations seemed to have even more resonance with their creators. They were David's Lou Reed and Matt's Andy Warhol. In a single sketch, a comedy legend was about to be born.

The thinking behind the first Lou and Andy scenes was typically bizarre. David had studied plenty of footage of the gravel-voiced American wild child Lou Reed – and decided to reinvent him as a deferential, lisping scruff from south London. As Andy Warhol (unaccountably Lou's lodger), Matt pulled on the wig he had used when singing songs on *Shooting Stars*, rolled out a Liverpool accent and started to sulk.

'If you have chips for your lunch you can't have them for your tea as well' Lou told his lodger.

'Yeah, I know. I want chips,' Andy replied, completely ignoring him.

As far as Matt and David were concerned, they had found their form. 'We liked those two characters right from the start. Something about them just seemed to fit; we could improvise with them straight away and even then we wanted to take them further,' says David. Little did he know, back in 2001, just how much further a reinvented Lou and Andy would ultimately go.

When *The Ralf Little Show* also came to a close, it looked as if *Rock Profile* and all of its characters might also have come to the end of the line, though. Matt and David had scored a cult success, but they were still a long way from the mainstream. Filming so many short sketches, and on such a shoestring budget, had been fun, especially as so many talented old friends had been drafted in to help. But it had also been frustrating. Everyone involved thought that the characters deserved a better showing. And Matt and David had never stopped thinking of new characters to play. Sometimes the stars they had put under their microscopes were too minor or had faded away too fast for a *Rock Profile*. Sometimes the way Matt and David wanted to play them didn't quite fit the interview-style format of the show. Some characters were simply based on people they saw in the street and had no connection to the music world. What they needed – as usual – was a different format. They wanted a whole new vehicle to show off some of these other creations.

Making tea in David's flat one afternoon, they started to talk about what, if anything, might connect all these disparate characters. They seemed to come from all over the country, from cities and towns, villages and suburbs. They were young and old, men and women, married and single, gay and straight. They might not be the kind of people who make Britain great, but they do make it very, very British. Could that be a way to connect them?

Having pulled together a range of scenarios, Matt and David put out some calls to try and place their new ideas. They wrote up a rough but passable version of a half-hour television show that featured this peculiar vision of Great Britain. And, just in case this didn't catch anyone's eye, they came up with a radio version of the same programme.

A little over a month after sending off the proposals, the men got a call from a radio producer at Broadcasting

House. He had their script in front of him. He wanted to talk about *Little Britain*.

CHAPTER 10

THE POWER OF RADIO

Taking a job on sleepy old Radio Four might have seemed like a backwards step for a pair of twenty-something comedians who had finally started to make real headway on television. But Matt and David had two very good reasons for signing up for this latest venture. Firstly, both of them had an encyclopaedic knowledge of broadcasting history – so they knew that radio was an ideal feeding place for hungry television producers. Ever since the BBC had started regular television broadcasts in 1936 it had been stealing formats, stars and whole shows from its radio arm – Matt and David both hoped that they might carry on the honourable tradition.

Secondly, both knew that, when it comes to comedy, Radio Four was very far from being sleepy. Young people might mock it as an anachronism, enjoyed only by the retired or the terminally uncool middle classes. But, like most professional comedians, Matt and David knew just how supportive it was of even the most outrageous new talents. Kenny Everett, Chris Evans and *Brass Eye*'s Chris Morris were just three big comedy names who had started their careers on the station. And shows from *Whose Line is it Anyway?*, *Room 101*, *Have I Got News For You*, *They Think it's All Over* and *Dead Ringers* all began on radio as well. More importantly for Matt and David, they knew that two of their comedy favourites, *The League of Gentleman* and *Goodness Gracious Me*, had both been heard on Radio Four long before making it on to prime-time television.

The experts confirmed that no aspiring comedian could afford to write off radio – though they were also keen to point out that there were no guarantees that a Radio Four show would be fast-tracked on to the small screen. 'It's not a formal arrangement. We wouldn't automatically say to a writer, "OK, you're going to be on telly, but first of all go and prove yourself on Radio Four,"' said BBC Head of Comedy Entertainment Jon Plowman – the man who spotted the potential of *Goodness Gracious Me* and gave it a radio slot so its creators could iron out any performance problems before its relaunch on BBC2. 'Not every show is suitable for both media, but when it does work it seems to work very well,' he says. 'The process of starting on radio is good for the BBC because it is a way of developing a format for a relatively small amount of money. And it good for the artists as well, because they get the confidence of doing six half-hours in front of a live audience – even if they are just mad, blue-rinsed old ladies that we've pulled in off Regent Street.'

Other broadcasters say that these same much-derided comedy audiences are actually ideal sounding blocks for new shows. 'Radio audiences are surprising. They understand satire, they don't seem to need huge stars, and they'll swallow amazingly experimental stuff. That's not true of mainstream television, and comedians can feel very exposed in the mainstream if they arrive there too early,' says producer Paul Schlesinger, who took the spoof documentary *People Like Us* from Radio Four to BBC2 in 1999.

Critic Rupert Smith argues that radio is a more 'intellectually rarefied' medium – which can be good news for even the most outrageous performers. 'There is more room for small-scale, cleverly written stuff that isn't judged solely on audience figures. Radio Four, in particular, has a clubby atmosphere about it; people who love it really love it, they buy into the station's world in a more thorough way than, say, viewers of BBC2. The rule, if there is one, seems to be that radio offers a home to untried talent because the stakes are lower, the failures less public. Try getting a drama commissioned for television and you will jump through a thousand hoops just to get a sniff of a green light. Pitch it to radio and you've a far greater chance of hitting the jackpot. When the commercial pressure is off a greater diversity of talent can flourish, unmolested by BARB figures and nervous controllers.'

Smith also had good news for people like Matt and David, who had seen their early bid for television fame destroyed by the critics. 'Radio is less subject to criticism, a new show won't be savaged by journalists, even if it is a bit ropey to start off with – writers and performers can learn on the job on radio. And, crucially, radio seems to offer a more liberal, laissez-faire environment. Comedy and drama can address a far wider and more challenging range of topics without getting the tabloids up in arms. Radio Four may seem like a cosy place, but never forget that it spawned *The Day Today* as well as the likes of *The League of Gentlemen.*'

And Matt and David certainly didn't forget this when they took that first call from the Radio Four producer about their embryonic sketch show, *Little Britain*. At this point, their proposal was still relatively loosely formed. But in essence they had decided to do a show that would take a virtual tour around the country, looking at all the people Matt and David had stored away in their minds in a lifetime of people-watching and simple nosiness. It would be British life, they said, but not as we know it. And it certainly wouldn't be described in a way the British Tourist Board might have hoped for.

The more people at Radio Four who looked at the initial proposal, the more green lights lit up. Everyone seemed to think this could work – and after yet another set of production meetings the pair got what they had been hoping for: a contract.

The deal was to produce a pilot show and four half-hour follow-ups. It certainly wasn't going to make Matt and David rich – looking back, they reckon they made an average of just £100 a week out of the contract once all the writing, rehearsal and performance time was taken into account. But back then money didn't matter. Both were prepared to take yet another loss-leading job in the hope that it would lead somewhere better.

The producers had given them roughly four months to write and record the shows – a relatively tough assignment that certainly got the adrenaline flowing. 'I haven't been so excited about anything we have done for a long time,' Matt told friends at the time. What both men enjoyed the most was the chance to dust down so many of their existing characters and put them in a bizarre new set of situations. And both felt an overwhelming sense of relief about being able to add life to other characters who had until now just been random jottings on a page. The men also swore not to go public with anything less than their absolute best. 'When we were working on the pilot show we wrote well over an hour's worth of material, recorded 45 minutes' worth, and then chose our favourite 28 minutes' worth for the final version. That's what we're planning to do with the rest of the series as well,' Matt said as their self-imposed start-date approached.

As it turned out, the adrenaline rush they got from signing the original contract meant they actually finished writing and recording a month ahead of schedule. At which point they decided to leave things well alone. 'With comedy, like any other form of writing, you can endlessly go back over things and make changes. But when you do so you can often iron out some of the life that you had in your original version. We decided that at a certain point you had to trust your earliest instincts, say enough, and walk away from it,' says Matt.

What reassured them hugely, though, was the reaction of the Radio Four audiences when the show was recorded. Being in the West End studios felt like a dream come true for both men – and for David in particular it felt a world away from his professional radio debut nearly a decade earlier on BBC Radio Bristol with the soon-forgotten *Bunce & Burner Visit Interesting Places*. Recording radio shows is, both say, like a more formal take on their original stand-up – because the performers are quite literally standing up on the stage in front of the bank of microphones. And they are very aware if the audience doesn't seem to be getting the jokes. What Matt and David had both told the producers from the start was that they wanted a real laughter track on the show – even if no one laughed and it ended up as quiet as the grave. They said having to use canned laughter would be an admission of failure. And fortunately, the question never arose. The early *Little Britain* audiences seemed to warm to the characters from the start. The laughter you can hear on the playbacks was all genuine, all recorded live in London.

The first set of radio sketches introduced some of the characters who would ultimately turn out to be national treasures. David's tragically bad transvestite Emily Howard was one of the first at the mike – 'I am not a man and never have been. I have a handkerchief,' she floundered as a former co-worker from the docks recognised her trying to rent a video. Then there was Matt's Vicky Pollard, talking the same gibberish, though not quite as fast as she would later in the series. There was Marjorie Dawes, caught in the cake aisle of her supermarket by a Fat Fighters member; there was Denver Mills, the woeful motivational speaker ('I won that race. I won a gold medal. I don't like to go on about it. But I did') and there was the world's most worrying masseur, Latymer Crown ('I'm going to ask you to focus on something relaxing. Imagine a gang of children throwing stones at a pensioner. He's weeping. Weeping softly').

It was on the final recording session that Matt and David finally allowed themselves to believe that they might have struck gold, however. 'It was when we played the Kenny Craig and the Michael and Sebastian sketches that there was a feeling in the room that something was really happening and that it could go somewhere. I felt that we had momentum and that if we were ever going to have a popular hit it would be with this,' says Matt. But would the show trigger the same responses more than a month later, when it finally went on air?

The first show was broadcast at 11pm on a Tuesday night in January 2001. Looking back, it might not seem like the highest-profile slot, but it was a good one for a new comedy. And straight away it was clear that the electricity the stars had felt in the radio studio was still sparking. The world hadn't been set alight. But Radio Four felt it had a hit on its hands – so it asked for more.

Getting commissioned for a second series means

several things: a little bit more money, a lot more credibility and a whole lot less worry. But for Matt and David it offered something else: a sense of affirmation. Yes, their Sir Bernard Chumley act had been rebooked at the Edinburgh Festival for three years running. But they were painfully aware that almost every other piece of professional work they had ever done had been a one-off. None of their pilot shows had been turned into a full series. Apart from *Rock Profile*, no first series had produced a second. Both men had started to worry that they were one-hit wonders – with an increasingly short shelf-life. A second radio series told them otherwise and the confidence this produced helped them to raise their games. The second Radio Four series got nominated for the annual Sony comedy award (the judges said that the show had 'truly original characters in a surreal parallel universe', though it ultimately lost out to the long-running *I'm Sorry I Haven't A Clue* when the first prize was handed out).

The second series was broadcast almost exactly a year after the first – four episodes were aired in February and March 2002. Again, the amount of time and effort the stars had put into it meant that on an hourly basis their fees didn't work out at much more than the minimum wage. And, because there were no guarantees that the radio show would lead anywhere, Matt and David both juggled a host of other projects around it. It meant a lot of long days and late nights as they tried to meet some very conflicting deadlines.

For his part, Matt had dusted down his pink romper suit, dragged his drums out of the cupboard and signed up for a new series of *Shooting Stars* as George Dawes – the first new shows in nearly four years. And in the summer of 2002 he was also cast in *Taboo*, a show that was being billed as one of the biggest musical launches of the year. Written by Boy George and broadly following his life story, it was jokingly referred to as 'a classic drags to bitches tale for all the family'. And while it included several of the best Culture Club songs, from 'Karma Chameleon' to 'Do You Really Want to Hurt Me?', it was still a big gamble for all concerned.

The first potential problem was the theatre itself – *Taboo* was being staged in The Venue, a former nightclub just off Leicester Square and not somewhere that the London theatre-going audiences were in the habit of visiting. The Venue itself wasn't designed like a traditional theatre either, something the producers tried to overcome by building much of the staging around a nightclub bar – which doubled up as the real bar during the interval.

The characters in the plot were certainly larger than life – as well as the Boy George figure, there was fellow pop star and sometime friend Marilyn, along with Steve Strange and the self-appointed fashion and style guru of the era, Leigh Bowery – played by Matt. The role involved a lot of Velcro and some precision 45-second costume changes (good practice for the manic *Little Britain* live show some three years later, Matt said). He got to sing one of the show's biggest, if most bizarre, numbers, 'Ich Bin Kunst' (I am Art), and Matt saw his character go from being the flamboyant leader of the music and performance art pack to being one of the country's earliest AIDS victims.

He gave the character everything he had and his portrayal was described by one fan as being a bizarre combination of 'a big, bald ball of glistening dough and a viciously camp Michelin man with shades of Hannibal Lecter' – if you can imagine Hannibal Lecter wearing lime-green tights and a top of matching feathers, that is. Funnily enough, some hard-core Lucas/Walliams fans said Matt's performance reminded them of something else as well – the weird, turquoise-coloured performance artist Vulva whom David had recently played in *Spaced*. For all the different career directions the pair appeared to take, something clearly kept on pulling them back together.

A raft of celebrities including Charlotte Church and Andrew Lloyd Webber were in the audience on *Taboo's* opening night and, while the show was largely panned by the critics, Matt was one of the few to scramble out of the wreckage with his reputation intact – even enhanced. 'He is a simultaneously compelling and repulsive portrayal of this walking freak show – and the best reason for seeing the show,' wrote Georgina Brown in the *Mail on Sunday*. 'All the performances are excellent, though all are eclipsed by Matt Lucas,' wrote her colleague Michael Coveney on the *Daily Mail*. And several months later, when Australian actor and comedian Mark Little took over the role, the compliments kept coming in for Matt.

Little was good 'but lacked the whiff of sulphur that Matt Lucas brought to the role', said the *Daily Telegraph*.

Years later, however, it would become clear that all had not been well behind the scenes at *Taboo*. Matt and Boy George, in particular, had not got along – largely due to the fact that George was happy for people to drink and smoke in the dressing room before the show when Matt thought everyone should keep their minds clear for the performance ahead. 'Thing got so bad he refused to even look at me, which was just as well as I didn't fancy being turned to stone,' Boy George said later of his younger co-star.

Fortunately, by the time his run in *Taboo* had ended, Matt got some fantastic news. Not only did he have a new job to go to, but it was the one he and David had been dreaming of for the past three years. With perfect timing they were told that the BBC had set aside the budget to film a pilot episode of *Little Britain*.

It turned out that, while Matt had been camping it up on stage as Leigh Bowery, the BBC executives had been locked in meetings trying to decide if the bizarre, character-based radio show really could survive the switch to the small screen. Everyone agreed it was a tough call – because for all the successful transfers from one medium to the other there has been an equal number of expensive failures. Experts say there are no guarantees that what seems like a sure-fire hit on radio will carry the same magic on to the screen. The legal comedy *Chambers*, a radio ratings topper of the late

1990s, is continually cited as an example. It had a huge fan base in its original format and got Sarah Lancashire to play the lead in the BBC1 transfer. At the time, she was fresh from *Coronation Street* and was one of the biggest stars on television. But even she couldn't inject enough magic into the transplanted show. The television version didn't work and ratings fell far short of even the pessimists' expectations. *After Henry* is another textbook example of a good show that can end up lost in translation. The gentle family-based comedy was perfect for the intimate world of radio. On television, it struggled to be noticed, despite taking its original star, Prunella Scales, with it and collecting a host of industry awards.

So would *Little Britain* win or lose if it did the transfer? After yet another lengthy meeting, the BBC execs decided to gamble on it being a winner. The money was raised for a pilot episode – and Matt and David both knew it was make-or-break time.

Their first task after signing the new contract (and opening a rare bottle of champagne) was to try and sign up as many top producers, directors and stage managers as possible. They wanted the best people around them – and it turned out they wouldn't have any problems attracting them. Graham Linehan, the writer and director of *Father Ted* and *Black Books*, was one of the first big names wanting to help out. 'I had heard the radio show and thought it was hilarious. David is one of the funniest people I know and Matt is perfect for a television sketch show – not least because he has absolutely no hair on his head so you can easily disguise him. His face is a brilliant blank slate for comedy.' Linehan was well aware of the perils of sticking too closely to the radio format if the show was to succeed in the new medium, however. 'I said they had to be careful not to have the sketches too based on dialogue once they got to television. I wanted them to think more in terms of visual jokes. You have to completely rethink and rebuild sketches for television.'

If strong visuals were what Linehan and others were after, then the naturally flamboyant David and the 'flamboyant-if-pushed' Matt were more than happy to oblige. Both knew exactly how to look larger than life on stage – and they were ready to do the same on screen. Linehan was overjoyed by their attitude and he was thinking big from the start.

'I felt Matt and Dave were far too funny to be kept a secret and I wasn't ever thinking of *Little Britain* as cult television. I wanted it to become a pure popular programme. We said we wanted it to be as big as the *Two Ronnies* or *Morecambe and Wise*. A traditional, old-fashioned sketch show, because there aren't any of those on television any more.'

Of course, Linehan did spot the fact that *Little Britain* wasn't always as cosy or traditional as the sketch shows of yesteryear – but he was convinced that its more modern feel was a selling point rather than a problem. 'It's nice to have some gay characters too, it's certainly a gayer sketch show than most,' he admitted in one of the biggest understatements of the time (David Baddiel famously said *Little Britain* was like 'A gay *Goodness Gracious Me*' and suggested they rename it *Goodness Gayness Me* and market it specifically at the gay market).

For all the laughs these sorts of comments triggered, Matt in particular was aware that they couldn't afford to alienate any potential viewers at this stage of their careers. 'The average age of our listeners on Radio Four was in the mid-fifties, so by going to television where the average would be half that we knew we had to do a different type of show from the start. But while we wanted to gain the younger viewers we wanted to keep the older audience on board as well. That was the balancing act.'

To help them achieve it, Matt and David called up a host of old friends. Producer Myfanwy Moore was vital to the project and carried on a working relationship that had already lasted nearly eight years. Lisa Cavalli-Green signed up again to do the men's make-up and styling, while Annie Hardinge was there for the costumes.

Former Doctor Who Tom Baker – one of Matt and David's childhood heroes – was sounded out about the ongoing job of recording the show's opening, closing and incidental voice-overs. Meanwhile, Bond theme composer David Arnold (the man behind the music in *Tomorrow Never Dies*, *The World is Not Enough* and *Die Another Day*) also agreed to follow up his work on the original radio series. He had become a good friend of the show's stars and they both knew he was essential to the overall feel of the project. The right music, the men knew, was one of the final pieces of the jigsaw that would subconsciously bind the show together. What we really want, Matt and David had said two years previously, was an iconic *Little Britain* sound. With David Arnold they found it – and as a laugh they gave him a host of cameo roles in the shows as an extra way of saying thanks.

Other people had an important, if more informal, influence on the vital pilot episode. One of them was photographer and film-maker Martin Parr, someone David in particular had long admired. Parr was himself a fan of Mike Leigh and the *Carry On* films – and he had a perfect eye for the minutiae of British society. 'We liked the fact that Martin Parr's work was incredibly colourful. He takes photos of poodles wearing pink bows or a woman's mouth with heavy red lipstick. They are the details we wanted to seek out and record ourselves,' said a hero-worshiping David. 'Overall, we looked at so many things back then. We wanted to create big characters but sustain an element of truth at the same time and we knew it wouldn't always be easy to get it right.'

It may be hard to remember now, but the sheer flamboyancy and large scale of the *Little Britain* pilot was something of a gamble back in 2002 when it was first being pulled together. Those were the years when television had decided that big was no longer beautiful – *The Royle Family* had started the new trend in the late 1990s, soon followed by the likes of *The Office* and *Phoenix Nights*. The kind of shows that were winning awards (and huge audiences) were those concentrating on small-scale, low-horizon, claustrophobic views of real-life homes and workplaces. Matt and David decided they would have to tackle the trend head on. Not for the first time in their lives, they were sure that being different could be a virtue. 'We looked at all those big hits like *The Office* and *Phoenix Nights* and realised how many shows there would be in their wake,' says David. 'We knew they would produce lots of naturalistic, moody performances which will end up as bad photocopies of the originals. So we really thought, We'll go ahead and go the other way instead with the pilot. Let's make it absurd. Let's do panto. Let's evoke the spirit of *The Two Ronnies*. We had a sense that people wanted a big, fun comedy show with wigs and costumes, the kind of show that hadn't been done for ages. And we weren't scared of doing it because we knew that was where our strength lies.'

'You can't top *Phoenix Nights* or *The Office*, so why try?' Matt asked rhetorically at the time.

When it came to putting the pilot episode together, Matt and David decided to follow the same pattern as they had on radio – they would write and prepare far more material than they needed so they had the luxury of picking the best for transmission. In the editing suite, they agonised over several scenes, before deciding upon the ones that would make – or break – their reputations. 'If you are making a series you are very aware that the first episode is the one that is going to get reviewed, so it has to be your best,' says David. 'If it's a pilot you know this is all the commissioning editors will ever see. So it has to have all your best stuff in it as well.' As the transmission date approached, Matt and David knew their choices mattered more than ever. But had they got them right?

CHAPTER 11

THE PILOT SHOW

'Britain. Britain. Britain. Population: one million. Number of towns: nine. Average height: thirty. Shoe size. But just who are Britain? Over the next eleventen weeks we aim to find out, by following the lives of ordinary British folk. What do they? Who is they? And why?' Tom Baker's voice boomed out over the opening credits of the pilot show, before the screen cut to the sight of a bewigged high-court judge lying on the steps of his courtroom and having a sneaky cigarette.

'British justice is the best in the world. Anyone who disagrees is either a gay, a woman or a mental.' With that, Tom led the show into the first full sketch – where the world would meet a certain Vicky Pollard. That initial scene said everything about how Matt and David saw what would become one of their most famous comic creations. She was on the spot, on the defensive and, mentally at least, on the run. 'With Vicky, the very best scenes are when she is just buying time until she can think of an excuse,' says David. So, 'Yeah, but no, but yeah,' fitted her like a glove as she desperately tried to find an answer to the questions she had been asked. 'Those words were never just a catchphrase,' says David. 'If they had been, the character wouldn't have worked for one sketch, let alone for so many. You can't just cynically think up catchphrases and then try and find a way to use them. They have to come out of who the character is and what they want to do and where they are. That's what happened with Vicky Pollard. She came first. The words came second.'

Next up in the pilot show came an early burst of surrealism – the initial version of the 'Ray McCooney' soup sketch, in which his diners squirmed in very British embarrassment as he punctuated the answers to their questions with some music and a jig. Also in the pilot were several scenes of the worrying masseur Latymer Crown (relatively easy to translate from radio), a new sketch in which Emily Howard tried to buy a ticket to her local swimming pool (of which more later) and the first of what would be many sketches in a shop. Matt says these Mr Mann scenes have always been among his favourites – in the first of them David's glum customer is looking for 'a pirate memory game suitable for children between the ages of four and eight'. As viewers would soon come to expect, he wouldn't find one.

The pilot had two scenes of the Prime Minister and his aide Sebastian – each of which would have been something of a surprise to Radio Four listeners, who had enjoyed the same characters nearly two years earlier. The difference was that for the television show Matt had given up the role of the Prime Minister and handed it to someone who would soon make it his own: Anthony Head.

Over the previous few years, Anthony had gone a long way from being best known as the star of the Gold Blend coffee adverts. He had been to Hollywood and reached millionaire and cult status after staring in the American teenage drama *Buffy the Vampire Slayer*. And his arrival on set as Prime Minister certainly gave the recording sessions a lift. 'It was exciting because there was a real gasp from the studio audience when Anthony joined us for his first recording,' says David. And he says there would be no prizes for guessing where the motivation for these particular sketches had come from. 'I don't think we could have written the sketch if John Major was still Prime Minister. It worked because for the first time we had a slightly dishy PM in Tony Blair. And because Peter Mandelson and Alistair Campbell both seemed a little too pleased with their closeness to the PM, which gave us the inspiration for the character of Sebastian. Having Anthony in the role was great because he has real status and gravitas. He made the perfect PM, came up with loads of ideas and was perfect at playing it straight, no matter how ridiculous everything got around him.'

In the pilot episode alone, he was prepared to drop his trousers and get up close and very personal with David's lovelorn Sebastian. And as he asked his fictional aide for the results of the latest approval ratings he forced himself not to laugh as Sebastian's character revealed his true feelings with the lines: 'They're very happy with your work on Northern Ireland. There's strong support for your health service reforms, they'd like to see you in shorts. They like the fact that you're assuming a tough stance on crime and they like it when your hair's a bit wet because you look kind of soppy, PM. They'd like to see you wrestle a man. Bosnia good. Education could do better. Wrestling men I've covered...'

Also in the pilot was the first Dennis Waterman sketch. Years earlier, Matt and David had found they were both huge *Minder* fans and for some reason they found it hilarious that the tough man in the title role also sang the show's theme tune. Even then the germ of an idea had been born. So years later, David took on and camped up the actor's persona, playing him as a theme-tune obsessed midget. While these sketches were heavy on the visuals, others in the pilot focused more on the characters, not least the initial Fat Fighters scene with Matt as group leader Marjorie Dawes.

This first scenario, which would be reshot for the end of the first series later that year, is the one most people associate with Matt's own childhood. In it Marjorie is 'welcoming' a chubby 13-year-old boy to the group – though Matt is adamant that nothing that happened next resembled his own childhood experiences at Weight Watchers. 'We're all friends, and we're all here to help each other,' Marjorie lies, before quizzing the boy relentlessly about all the name-calling she was convinced that he must suffer at school.

'What do they call you? The Incredible Bulk? Piggy? Pigs in Space? Chubby checker? Fat greedy boy? Cracker?' she screeched, with increasing desperation.

'They don't all make fun of me being fat.'

'No, but the others will be thinking it,' she told him, before lashing out when one of the group gently suggests he shouldn't eat so much chocolate.

'What do you mean don't eat too much chocolate? All the other kids hate him. Chocolate is the only friend he's got.'

The final two sketches Matt and David selected for the pilot featured Daffyd in his Welsh pub and teenage Jason meeting his friend's nan in their council flat. Matt and David had huge hopes for both these scenarios and had already written several more scenes for the characters. Whether they would ever get the chance to film them would all depend on how well that pilot episode went. And after the excitement of putting that first show together, both men suddenly admitted that they were overcome with doubts.

Both were convinced that their pilot show was good enough to win a full commission. But both knew full well that they had been here before. One previous sitcom pilot they had filmed, *Crazy Jonathan's*, had got to the same stage, only to disappear without trace. 'After so many years of work, we felt we were in last-chance saloon with *Little Britain*. So much that we had done had come close but never made the final breakthrough. It felt like our last roll of the dice,' said David as the transmission date for the pilot approached.

What made the pair even more nervous was the fact that their pilot show was only going to make it on to mainstream television by default. BBC2, the key comedy channel they were hoping to attract, hadn't commissioned it. Instead, the money had come from the brand-new digital channel BBC3. And, in 2003, this wasn't exactly the ideal place to be if you wanted to make it big in British television. 'Viewing figures suggest the BBC's digital channels are watched by three amnesiacs and a drunk who fell asleep and rolled over on to the remote control,' wrote *The Times'* television critic Paul Hoggart shortly after they were launched. 'A couple of drunks and a budgie' was another equally uncharitable assessment of the channel's audience and influence.

But, for all that, the new digital channels did offer a once-in-a-lifetime opportunity for people like Matt and David – because in some ways BBC3 could have been set up with them in mind. In 2000, when the replacements to the ailing arts channel BBC Choice had first been mooted by Director General Greg Dyke, the idea had been for a third channel that would be aimed squarely at the youth market. Culture Secretary Tessa Jowell refused the application, saying that the under-25s were already well catered for elsewhere. So, after a new application process, the BBC had come up with plans for a revised output aiming at the slightly older 25- to 34-year-old demographic – which included most of the audiences of the live comedy clubs where Matt and David were still playing. The government had given the new proposal the green light, but only after the BBC had agreed to a range of tough new conditions. Top of the list was the requirement that 80 per cent of the channel's shows had to be new, specially commissioned and high-quality output – a bid to ensure that the channel was not just used as a dumping ground for repeats of American sitcoms and cop dramas.

The requirement was a boon for independent producers in Britain and the rest of Europe – from where Jowell said 90 per cent of the shows had to originate. 'BBC3 will be packed full of modern, radical, imaginative and funny British shows,' the BBC directors said in the pre-publicity for the launch. And it was on this channel that *Little Britain* was getting its first showing.

Two Johnnys – Johnny Vaughan and Matt and David's old writing partner Johnny Vegas – were the first faces on BBC3 when it finally went live on 9 February 2003. 'This channel is a facet of the BBC and the BBC is paid for through the government and the government is voted in by you – so if this is crap it is your fault,' Johnny Vegas said in the opening moments of the broadcast. He then introduced some big stars including Justin Timberlake, the Appleton sisters and Dermot O'Leary. And then they cued the start of *Little Britain*.

As it turned out, the audience was small, even though the channel's opening night was being shown simultaneously on BBC2. At little more than 125,000, the number of viewers that Matt, David and all their characters were estimated to have attracted that night was statistically little more than zero. But behind the scenes something interesting was happening. A small but significant number of people actually rang the BBC to say how good the show had been and asking when they could see more of it. A near-simultaneous repeat of the Radio Four shows turned out to attract more rather than less listeners second time around – and the second series was also being nominated for more radio awards. A buzz was being created and this worked as a minor wake-up call to the corporation's top brass. Could they have a home-grown hit on their hands?

A tiny number of key television critics said that the answer was an emphatic yes – and once more Victor Lewis-Smith was one of them. Abandoning his once critical stance, he described Matt and David as 'The brilliant comedic talents behind *Rock Profile*' and said *Little Britain* was 'A splendidly original take on contemporary British life. Surreal comedy is usually very easy to create and very hard to watch, but this succeeded magnificently because it wasn't whimsical and meandering but had hard satirical targets (and lots of men dressed as women) in the best traditions of Monty Python. This has all the makings of a comic masterpiece, being truly innovative and funny and very, very British.'

Others said the pair were the natural 'heirs to Dick Emery', which they took as high praise. The *Sunday Times* was another of the show's early champions. '*Little Britain* makes the move from Radio Four with real aplomb and if anyone has features and an economy of facial gesture more finely nuanced for sketch-based visual comedy than Matt Lucas then possibly it is his partner, David Walliams,' wrote its television reviewer in February 2003. 'Be the first to catch this successor to *The Fast Show* from the start,' he urged.

At home with the Sunday papers, Matt and David were jubilant. If they really were to be a worthy successor to *The Fast Show*, they would need to be offered a series, rather than a one-off pilot show. Support in the newspapers could make that happen. They carried on talking to their producers, fine-tuning their characters, reimagining them for television rather than radio and inventing as many new visually based jokes as possible. If a series did get the green light, everyone was determined to be ready for it.

Well, everyone but David. Just before the pilot show had been put together, he had teamed up with *Human Remains* writer and star Rob Brydon. The pair, who had worked together on *Cruise of the Gods*, had come up with an idea for a new sitcom of their own. Due to be called *Home*, it was to have been set in an old people's home and Ronnie Corbett, Bob Monkhouse and some of the other old-school comedians the men had admired since childhood were being lined up for the leading roles. If it had taken off, then David's partnership with Matt could be about to hit the rocks – and *Little Britain* could have been strangled at birth.

Rob certainly seemed keen to get the new double act up and running. 'Even in the early stages of *Home* when we only had sessions improvising the characters, David has had me in hysterics,' he said. 'Usually when I work I am not the one who is corpsing. I'm a bit dour in that way. David actually ended up making me feel so unfunny because he is so bloody funny. I came back from filming *Cruise of the Gods* with him saying he was the funniest man in the world and he still is.'

But, fortunately for Matt, David and Rob's sitcom never got beyond the early stages. And Rob, for one, was ready to admit that the Lucas/Walliams roadshow might be unstoppable. He had been to the editing suite to watch some of the early scenes from the *Little Britain* pilot and was convinced it was a classic – and that the pair would soon be back together working on a full series. 'There is a delicious quality to the show,' he said. 'There's a hint of something seedy, which I quite like. What they are doing has both a warmth and a touch of the bizarre.' He said he would put money on the pilot being picked up for a series. And, needless to say, he would have won his bet.

The call and the contract came through in the late spring of 2003. The BBC wanted at least eight episodes – and they wanted them ready to be broadcast on BBC3 that September. Matt and David were both ecstatic and terrified. This was what they had spent the past decade hoping for. Now they had less than six months to deliver it. The heat was on – and the problems started straight away.

The first stumbling block came when the men called their director, Graham Linehan, to tell him the good news. Graham's early confidence in the project meant he wasn't surprised, but when he looked at his work diary he realised there was no way he could work on a full series in the next six months.

Frantically hitting the phones to find out who might be available, the men suddenly got lucky – Steve Bendelack, the director whose career had begun on *Spitting Image* and who had since worked on everything from *French and Saunders* and *The Royle Family* to *The League of Gentleman* wasn't just available, he was jumping at the chance to take over Linehan's role. Bendelack reckoned that the whole shape and feel of *Little Britain* was in tune with his comedy brain and he was determined to make it a success. Matt and David met up with him and loved his plans to bring a real 'cinematic' feel to the series.

'He was the one who gave the show an epic feel,' says a grateful Matt. 'As David always said, we wanted to do what it says on the tin with the title. And Steve was able to bring a sweeping, grand sense that we really did travel around the country in the show.'

Other strong supporters also signed up as news of the commission gained ground. David's fellow *Doctor Who* fan Mark Gatiss was fresh from writing and performing in *The League of Gentlemen* and was widely seen as being at the top of his comedy game. So the men were jubilant when he agreed to be *Little Britain*'s first script editor.

Myfanwy Moore, Lisa Cavalli-Green and a host of others from the pilot episode were also signing up for the series, along with all the key performers. So the big task was to write and polish up four hours' worth of top-notch scripts. And here the men learned some tough new rules of television comedy.

The first was that money (or the lack of it) talks, even when you have a major commission under your belt. Financial reasons meant some of Matt and David's favourite sketches and characters had to be dropped, while others had to be expanded. The Britannia Cat Club and the Witches House were both pretty much dropped because they were too expensive to film, for example. By contrast, the Kelsey Grammar School sketches were expanded for television in order to keep the budget on track. 'Once you've built the whole set and got a roomful of child actors there, you need to fill more than just two minutes of screen time to justify the costs,' says David. It was an early lesson for both men that, even with budgets approaching £350,000 per half-hour episode (more than a hundred times their budget for *Rock Profile*), their television comedy still had to keep its feet on the ground.

Fortunately, Matt and David remained entirely grounded in the writing process. They decided that the best way to get the first series written was to stick to the tried-and-tested formula of spending long days in each other's flat. In the past they had always treated comedy writing like any other full-time occupation. Nothing was going to change now they were finally approaching the big time.

'People say that we must think up our ideas down the pub, but in reality the shows are powered by peppermint tea at home,' is David's now famous description of their working practice. 'It's one of us on the sofa, one of us on the computer. And it is hard work.'

What also kept things real was the fact that until very recently the pair would still get to each other's flat by bus – and even this short commute could raise a laugh when they describe it to others. 'I'm always very grand when I get on the bus,' says Matt. 'I say, "First Class, my man." As loud as I can.'

'And I'm like those women who say, "Thank you, driver," as if the man driving the bus is their own personal chauffeur,' claims David.

But once they have got to their destination they get a lot more serious. Five days a week they stay locked up together from 9 till 5 with a microwave meal from Marks & Spencer for lunch – a small but significant step up from the garage-bought sandwiches they had eaten when filming *Rock Profile*. 'The blank page and the empty computer screen are the most terrifying things in the world,' David says of the early days of writing *Little Britain*. 'As all writers will say, you have to force yourself sometimes, and writing on your own is not very enjoyable, which is why it is great that we have each other. You need someone there to say if something is funny or not and while it is an intense way of working it needs to be sociable.'

Matt was equally emphatic about how hard they worked – and how much they relied on each other to produce their best work. 'The whole show is written together, absolutely everything together. We treat it like a job, and there's never a sense that we don't fancy it today. By the time we did *Little Britain*, we had been working together for some eight and a half years, which is a long time for two people who are essentially stuck in a room together. The longest we have been apart was probably when Dave went off to do *The Cruise* with Steve Coogan.'

Their first task in 2003 was to work out which characters and scenes from the radio show could be used on television and which had to be created from scratch. When making the decisions they relied on their belief that British audiences seemed to have a strange affinity for the grotesque. In real life we might all run a mile from the likes of Tony Hancock, Alf Garnett, Mr Rigsby, Basil Fawlty, Alan Partridge and David Brent. But it seems we can't get enough of them on our small screens. Other comedy giants agree that characters and subjects that most people see as off-limits can make great humorous creations. 'We all have good thoughts and bad thoughts. But nobody expresses the bad thoughts. We just think them and don't say them. But the bad thoughts are funny,' says legendary *Seinfeld* creator Larry David.

Fortunately, neither Matt nor David had any problems putting bad thoughts down on paper. Getting strong and true characters was the foundation of all the work the pair did. And they didn't care where they found them – they likened the process to lifting up the paving stones of British national life to see what kind of odd little creatures crept out. Having found and fashioned these creatures, it was always all the better if they saw their outsider status as entirely natural, and if they wore their eccentricity as a badge of honour. Monsters, disguised as ordinary members of the public, were the most attractive discoveries of all. So it was an easy decision for Matt and David to bring Sir Bernard Chumley back into the frame, though taken out of his old settings and replanted in a council flat with a disabled sister always just off camera.

Marjorie Dawes, Ray McCooney, Sebastian Love, Daffyd Thomas, Vicky Pollard, Emily Howard, Andy and Lou and hypnotist Kenny Craig also got the thumbs-up for early sketches in the first series – and Matt and David say that, once the characters had been born, their sketches and the jokes should flow automatically. 'It is about looking for something interesting and then the funny bit just usually happens naturally. The characters have to grow organically,' says Matt. But for all his confidence, he also admitted that he lay awake at nights terrified that inspiration might not strike, and that the characters might have nowhere convincing to go. Past experience told him he needed to relax. 'Worrying endlessly about the one gag that didn't work was always my downfall when I was on the stand-up circuit. It helps a lot to be more relaxed about that kind of thing and I am gradually getting there,' he said, as the first *Little Britain* deadlines approached.

Equally under pressure, David tried to remind himself

that comedy didn't have to be rocket science – and that inspiration could hit at any time. 'The best sketches we write are the ones we write really quickly. We never sit down and think, What shall we satirise today? We just try to be funny.' As part of that job, the pair also spent time discussing and relearning lessons from every comedy hero they had ever had as children, everyone who had made a success of their careers since and everyone the pair had worked with to date.

David says he took heart from the way Steve Coogan had created and played Alan Partridge – refusing to patronise the character and refusing to hold back from making him entirely dislikeable. Matt, meanwhile, looked back to the way Vic Reeves and Bob Mortimer had worked when he had first filmed with them as an angry teenager. In particular, he admired the speed with which they kept the humour coming – and so in *Little Britain* he vowed that viewers should hardly ever have to wait more than 15 seconds for a laugh. By the middle of the summer, the key scripts for the whole first series had been written and as for the radio show Matt and David felt they had to trust them rather than endlessly tamper with them. It was time for the cameras to roll.

Looking back, the men say the sheer scale of filming a BBC production both excited and scared them. It was such a different world to the low-rent existence they had occupied to date. And once they got used to the crowds of people in every meeting and on every set they started to relax and enjoy it. 'The crew always laughs when Matt comes out of wardrobe. They hardly ever do when I appear,' joked David when asked about the atmosphere in the studio.

The process of filming was roughly divided into two halves. For nearly seven weeks, they went out on the road with a full crew for the various location shoots, before heading back to the studio for the interior and linking scenes. On location, Matt and David had to get used to a series of very early starts instead of the traditional late nights of the stand-up comedy clubs. And it was following one of these first early starts that a minor comedy legend was born.

It happened during the filming of what was to become one of the most famous and frequently repeated scenes in the whole show – when Lou takes Andy to the swimming pool and speaks to the lifeguard at great length about how much help his charge may require getting into and out of the pool. While talking, Lou misses the fact that Andy has actually left his chair, stormed up to the top diving board, jumped into the pool, swam to the side and got back, dripping, into his former position before Lou turns around.

'Did you shower?' he asks absent-mindedly, as he prepares to get Andy ready for his swim.

Apart from appreciating the joke itself, the television professionals on the *Little Britain* shoot took notice of the fact that this complex scene was filmed in a single take, first time around. Matt and David were marked out as fellow pros from then on. They had earned some real respect in the industry. And, consequently, everyone felt more confident about the whole venture.

With the location work finished, the team had an intensive series of five-day studio shoots for Daffyd's 'Scarecrow and Mrs King' pub scenes, Sebastian's political scenes and all the other interiors. Between the sketches, the producers played the recorded location footage on big screens to the audience in the studio, so the laughter heard on the final show is genuine rather than canned – just as it was on their radio show.

And all the time Matt and David were buzzing around the set, worrying, working, keeping the audience amused and polishing their production until it shone. It's an experience both of them thrive on. 'Because we have both done so much live comedy we work well in front of an audience and enjoy the atmosphere you get out of it. When you have an audience there, you know straight away what works and what doesn't, which is invaluable,' says Matt. 'We wanted to stick with that on the show as much as possible.' Everyone else agreed. Actress Ruth Jones, who played the barmaid in the Daffyd sketches, says it had been years since she had performed in front of a live audience – but she too soon realised how useful it was to have instant feedback about how well your lines were going.

Meanwhile, Matt and David carried on joking. Is it different filming for television compared to recording for radio, they were asked at one point. 'The Nan and Jason sketches are different because on the radio I didn't have to actually perform any sexual acts with her,' says David.

'No, but you still did,' countered Matt.

The other confidence-boosting feature of the shoot was that so many of the old-timers who had been in the radio series had remained on board, and several other top performers had signed up as well. Tom Baker was a case in point. Persuading him to work on the radio show some three years earlier had taken time. Keeping him for the television pilot and the whole first series was a lot easier, because by then Tom had become a huge fan of the comedy and of its creators. 'Matt and David are just very funny together, quite outrageous, but such nice people. My job on the show is to be so silly and overemphatic that anyone who is offended is revealed to have no sense of humour,' he said of his role in the show. And as the weeks passed it seemed there were no lines too ridiculous (or too suggestive) for him to speak.

'Tom is just brilliant,' says Matt, who jokes that if the former Doctor Who hadn't been available they would have gone for Harold Pinter or Mr Bronson from *Grange Hill*. 'He has this very authoritative voice, but a kind of fruitiness and an absurd almost supernatural streak. You can make him say absolutely bizarre things and he will say them with total authority.'

And bizarre they were. 'Working-class people in Britain are stored in buildings like these,' Tom said over establishing shots of a tower block. The line 'Sheltered accommodation is where people who are too old and lazy to do things for themselves are kept' leads into a Jason and Gary sketch, while a Vicky Pollard episode is introduced with: 'Swimming pools in Britain have very strict rules: no bombing, no petting, no ducking and no fondue parties.' Amazingly, considering they were still relatively untried talents, Matt and David had managed to sign up a host of other high-profile names for the shows as well – even though many of the established performers knew from the start that they were only there to be humiliated. David Soul had a cameo playing himself as a hospital visitor while Jennie Bond was there in her royal reporter's role. *Are You Being Served?* star Mollie Sugden was also ready to send herself up (and end up getting killed), while Anthony Head still dominated the series as the Prime Minister.

Judging by the audience reaction in the studio, the sketches were pushing all the right buttons, especially when some of the guest stars were on set. Everyone also seemed to appreciate being let in to some trade secrets, such as the fact that two of the extras in a Des Kelly scene were Matt's mother and stepfather, making their professional debuts. David's mother, not to be left out, was a frequent visitor to the set as well, and she brought homemade cakes for the crew. Her other claim to fame was that she had provided the inspiration for the Mollie Sugden sketches after coming back from a weekend away having met a woman who really had been boasting about being the actress's bridesmaid.

Filming ended and the long process of editing began in the late summer of 2003. Matt, David and the rest of the production team had the tough task of deciding which sketches to use, which to ditch and how to pace each episode. What they had promised from the start was that, if the studio audience hated a sketch, they would drop it immediately. But as it turned out that wasn't a problem. They ended up with too much for the first series, so as the final edits were signed off they were convinced that the end result was as strong as it could be. They were also aware of just how far they had travelled and how close they were to really making it. The struggling comics from the stand-up circuit, whose first big break on the BBC had been killed off some four years earlier, had finally got another BBC series in the bag. And this time they were convinced that the critics couldn't destroy them.

The first show was broadcast at 9pm on Tuesday, 16 September 2003 on the fledgling BBC3. And audiences and critics alike gave it a big thumbs-up. 'In *Little Britain*, both Matt Lucas and David Walliams have revealed a Baroque talent for creating outrageous characters. If the new series builds on the strength of the opening show then it should fly and we will be hearing impressions of Vicky and Daffyd from every joker in the country,' wrote Paul Hoggart in *The Times* – billing the show as classic 'water-cooler television' that would thrive as word of mouth in workplaces and schools helped it build its audience. To his credit, Victor Lewis-Smith in London's *Evening Standard* was back yet again to admit he had gone from being the pair's fiercest critic to becoming their biggest fan. 'The erstwhile untalented Walliams and unfunny Lucas are now two of the hottest comedy properties on television. Now will somebody remove this sword from me?' he wrote, having figuratively thrown himself upon it.

From the producer down, everyone connected to *Little Britain* was jubilant. All their money and effort had been well spent. And within weeks of the first BBC3 broadcast the BBC made an announcement that would mean even more. The corporation announced that, as the show was getting such a strong audience on BBC3, it could have that one final push towards the mainstream. Matt and David had made it back on to BBC2. They had gone from stand-up, to national radio, to digital television, to a full terrestrial broadcast. It had been an incredible journey. And, as events would prove, it was only the beginning.

Meanwhile, a sometimes unlikely band of other commentators were also lining up to give the pair all the vital pre-publicity and support they needed. The *Mail on Sunday* is famous as the chief advocate of the Middle England that Matt and David's characters were so quick to send up. But it was first in line with the compliments: 'The year's hottest television show and that rare thing – a new comedy that feels like a classic... Until now it has been a hidden gem tucked away on the BBC's youth channel BBC3. But as it rapidly turns into a bona fide comedy cult, the schedulers have cleared a slot for it on BBC2 from where its camp catchphrases are sure to find their way into the nation's pub conversations.'

As the catchphrases started to do just that, Matt and David found their way into some pretty exalted company as well. Matt clapped like a man possessed when David was named Best Newcomer at the 2003 British Comedy Awards (in the year when Steve Coogan and Ronni Ancona got Best Comedy Actor and Actress Awards and *Coupling* was named Best TV Comedy). 'Comedy is in rude health with a new generation emerging who are mixing old-fashioned *Carry On* vulgarity and new-wave surrealism,' said commentator Bruce Dessau, as the awards were handed out. Magazines were also taking notice of the comedians. The pair were voted *GQ*'s Comedians of the Year, and got Men of the Year awards from *Arena* and 'Lafta' awards from *loaded*.

It seemed as if nothing could go wrong as their BBC2 launch approached. Or could it? On the positive side, it seemed that with *The Office*, *Phoenix Nights* and *The League of Gentlemen* at the end of their runs there didn't seem to be a great deal of tough competition in the adult comedy market – no one really felt Robert Lindsay and Zoë Wanamaker's show *My Family* or Ardal O'Hanlon's equally family-friendly *My Hero* were exactly at the cutting edge of cool, for a start.

But, more worryingly, there was a sense that the pair were getting their big break just as television comedy faced its biggest challenges. 'Is it all over for sitcoms?' one newspaper asked as the reality-television revolution gathered momentum and a host of traditional comedies were axed or shunted on to graveyard slots after just a couple of weeks of poor ratings. As a sketch show rather than a traditional sitcom, was Matt and David's baby going to fare better or worse in this new comedy climate?

Nobody knew for sure. But one thing was very clear – however few comedy rivals they had, the nature of modern television meant that instant good reviews and powerful momentum were vital if Matt and David's big career leap was to end safely. Both knew how, in a gentler age, the BBC had given its biggest radio star – Tony Hancock – a near limitless amount of leeway when *Hancock's Half-Hour* made the leap on to television. 'In 1956 Tony Hancock as "the lad himself" certainly looked the part of his grumpy radio persona – a prince turned into a frog who had just realised that no amount of kissing was going to reverse the transformation,' says media expert Ian Johns of that uncertain transition. 'But on screen the patter seemed forced and the visual gags were often lamely grafted on. It was only by series four or five that it all became a triumph. Series seven, by then called simply *Hancock*, included the episodes 'The Radio Ham' and 'The Blood Donor' and only then provided British comedy with some of its finest half-hours.'

In 2003, there was zero chance that the corporation would offer such an extended honeymoon period in the hope that any of its new stars could one day come up with the goods. Matt and David were in no doubt whatsoever that they had to get laughs, viewers and comedy credibility right from the word go. The 10pm

BBC2 slot they had been given for *Little Britain* was a tough one – and on their first night they were up against Uma Thurman and British star-of-the-moment Jude Law in the television premier of *Gattaca*. Everyone knew that the pressure was on.

CHAPTER 12

CREATING VICKY POLLARD

'Yeah, but no, but yeah, but no, but yeah.' Vicky Pollard was the first of the major characters that mainstream Britain would see when the show finally made it to BBC2 at the end of 2003. She might have horrified a fair few of them. But she certainly struck a chord from the word go.

The original scene of Vicky in court, recorded in the pilot episode, was not shown until later in that first series. Instead, her initial appearance would be in school, with David playing her long-suffering teacher. As usual, his questions about her work were soon drowned out by Vicky's stream-of-consciousness self-justification. As one critic commented, she's not rambling, she's going on a 100-metre sprint – in more than one direction at once.

Vicky's extraordinary gabble is incoherent, unpunctuated and apparently meaningless. But it is also comic genius – and tightly scripted from the start. Whether it's 'She's the one what done the thing about that thing if she gives sweets don't eat 'em 'cos she's dirty' or 'He fingered Carly down the back of the ice rink', there is something extra in the lines that keeps them alive long after their speaker has finally been forced to draw breath.

The character of Vicky Pollard was born when Matt showed David the old video he had filmed as part of his Bristol drama course – in which he had asked members of the public how they were , let the camera roll and captured their responses. Sitting together in David's north London flat, nearly a decade later, they watched the teenage lad who couldn't navigate through even the simplest of sentences – yet who was determined to try and was convinced that he had something important to say. It was the look in his eyes that got them, the slight desperation of someone who started sentences with no real idea of how they might end. They loved the lad's flat West Country accent, the way he dressed, the way he stood. They were convinced that he could be a classic comedy character and there and then both tried to imitate him and bring him alive.

Unfortunately, the more they tried, the more they felt something was missing. So after a while they moved on to other things – which was when they saw an iconic *Time Out* magazine cover featuring two teenage girls on a day out in Brighton. Nikki Carpenter and Stacey Bennett were in tracksuits, with plenty of eye make-up and scraped-back hair. A light bulb went off in Matt's head the moment he saw them.

'Let's make him a girl,' he said of their half-formed character. And so, keeping the West Country accent intact, he gave it a try. David laughed out loud and Vicky Pollard was born.

But, as with every other *Little Britain* sketch, the basic character was just the start. What matters more, and what makes the sketches work, is the context in which the characters are placed and the subliminal history they are given. Their creators get particularly angry when their characters are attacked as one-dimensional or as 'a gallery of grotesques with randomly selected quirks thrown in', as one critic wrote. Instead, they say that every part of their characters have been researched and written down. We might only be seeing one side of them, they say. But the rest is all there for anyone who takes the time to look.

'With Vicky Pollard, we took a lot of care in putting all the right references in,' says David. 'We think of all the names of her friends, boys she fancies, places she goes. She's not just in a sports shop, as an example, she's in Foot Locker. And her friends aren't called Mary and Jane, they are called Destiny, Shannon and Bethany. It is also incredibly carefully observed in terms of the way girls of that age look, how they put their eye liner on and how they put their lip liner on. We want all our characters to have an iconic feel to them, to be immediately recognisable in the way they look.'

And that was absolutely true of Vicky – who was a

zeitgeist figure from the start. 'You can be really lucky and come up with the right character at the right time. Like Harry Enfield with "Loadsamoney" or with Ali G,' said Matt. 'There is a sense now that there are Vicky Pollards on every street corner and that it was just luck that got us there before anyone else. But in reality we had seen a seed of an idea very early on and spent a lot of time and effort developing it.'

Matt also had to spend a huge amount of time preparing for each Vicky Pollard scene – because from an actor's point of view she is one of the hardest characters in the business to crack. 'You have to really, really know the lines,' says Matt. 'It is all tightly scripted and there is no improvisation. Though it can sometimes feel as if it needs 40 takes to get it all right.'

And, if you don't believe him, then try this quick burst from one of Vicky's most popular scenes for yourself. She's in the supermarket, having been accused of shoplifting. And she's not happy: 'No but yeah but no but yeah because I was just about to do it if you have waited. God this is so unfair I ain't ever even nicked nuffin' or nuffin' this is like being back at Borstal honestly if anyone's nicked anything it's Michelle Pope because we were all at the leisure centre and Michelle Pope put her hand up the chocolate machine to try and pinch a packet of Payne's Poppets but she got her hand stuck in I tried to cut it off with a pen knife and she completely had an eppy and said that Mr Bailey was right I am educationally subnormal but anyway don't listen to her because

Above: With *The Office* star Ricky Gervais at the 2004 BAFTA Awards where Matt and David won the Best Comedy Performance award.

Below: With television presenters Ant and Dec at the British Comedy Awards. They picked up a staggering three gongs on the night, beating Ricky Gervais's *The Office* to the top prizes.

And the accolades just keep coming…

Above left: At the 2005 BAFTA Awards, winning the Best Comedy Performance and Best Comedy Programme awards.

Above right: When the boys couldn't make it to the 2005 National Television Awards, they sent their mothers along to take their place – Matt's mother Diana (left) and David's mother Kathleen (right).

Below: With friend Robbie Williams at the GQ Men of the Year Awards.

Matt and David's trip to Africa for Comic Relief in 2005 proved to be a life-changing experience for the pair, driving them to become more involved with charity work.

Above left: Matt with Comic Relief mastermind Lenny Henry at the Red Nose Day launch.

Above right: Matt with (clockwise from top left): Elle MacPherson, television presenter June Sarpong, Dawn French, *Blue Peter* presenter Konnie Huq and Davina McCall.

Below: As Andy and Lou at Live 8.

Lay-dees' man: David Walliams has been linked with a string of high profile women:

Above left: Singer and model Lisa Moorish, ex-girlfriend of Liam Gallagher and Pete Doherty.

Above right: With Dannii Minogue.

Below left: With model and George Clooney's on-off girlfriend Lisa Snowdon.

Below right: With Denise Van Outen.

Above: The morning after the night before – David and Patsy Kensit leave her London home separately.

Below: Getting cosy with television star Abi Titmuss. The pair were together for nearly four months – something of a record for David in recent times.

Above left: Matt with his boyfriend, television producer Kevin Mcgee – the couple do their best to remain out of the public eye. Unlike David who simply loves the celebrity party circuit:

Above right: With the *Mirror*'s notorious gossip columnists - the 3am girls.

Below left: With Elton John's boyfriend David Furnish and photographer Sam Taylor Wood

Below right: With *Eastenders*' Shane Richie. David is a huge fan of the show and was delighted to play Shane's onscreen best friend. 'It was a dream come true,' he declared.

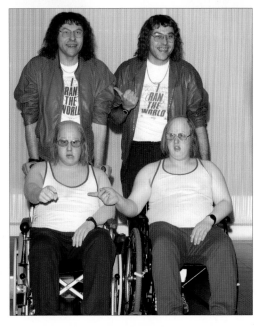

Above left: David at another premiere, with *Shaun of the Dead* and *Spaced* star Simon Pegg and *Star Wars* director George Lucas. Both David and Matt had worked with Simon before and were interested in branching out into other areas.

Above Right: The boys courted controversy once more with the third season of *Little Britain* – the character of the incontinent old lady Mrs Emery angered many viewers and critics.

Below left: David's home 'Supernova Heights', which formerly belonged to Oasis star Noel Gallagher.

Below right: At the unveiling of their Andy and Lou waxworks at Madame Tussaud's.

Above: Matt and David's infamous appearance on the *Parkinson Show*, where David danced with pop star Will Young before faking a kiss with him and sitting him on his knee.

Middle: Switching on the Christmas lights with Madonna and Stella Mccartney at her shop.

Bottom: Bringing down the house – the *Little Britain* live show was a huge success. Where David and Matt go from here only they know, but their future certainly looks bright.

everyone knows she done it with an Alsatian.' Most of us would probably need at least another 39 takes to get it fast enough. Especially while staying in character, being dressed as a teenage girl and staring directly at a David Walliams who is desperately trying not to laugh.

'The way Vicky speaks is a modern phenomenon,' says David, who says he struggles scene after scene to keep a straight face in front of Matt's Vicky. 'Ten years ago, you couldn't have done her because ten years ago people constructed proper sentences.' What makes Vicky an even stronger character, though, is that there is more to her than just these rapid-fire monologues. Matt and David change the pace by writing short, traditional comedy lines for her as well, adding more depth to her in the process.

'Get out of the pool and get changed,' David's lifeguard tells her, in an early scene filmed in the same Morden public pool where he had been taken by his grandfather as a child.

'I'll just have a wee first then I'll get changed,' Matt's Vicky replies from the pool.

'Don't you want to pass your GCSE, Vicky?' he asks her in another scene, this time in the part of her exasperated teacher.

'My GCS what?' she replies, utterly in character.

And then, of course, there is one of the most quoted Vicky Pollard moments of all. This time David is playing a social worker trying to find out what has happened to her baby. It turns out that Vicky has swapped it for a Westlife CD. How could she do something like that?

David asks. 'I know, they're rubbish,' is all Vicky can offer in her defence.

For all the jokes and the one-liners, Matt says it is simple hard work that brings characters like Vicky to life. 'Performing comedy is a surprisingly tense business and you are on a knife edge between success and failure most of the time,' he says. David adds that if you want to make it work you also need to know how to act, as well as how to act the fool. 'In the sketch when I am attracted to Matt's grandma, it's no use my playing it like I'm in a comedy scene. I have to play the situation as real because the best comedy always has a kind of truth about it,' he says of his role as Jason. Outsiders agreed that both men had the talent to know when to hold back and when to let rip. 'The series succeeds because its stars are accomplished straight actors as well as gifted writers,' says critic Victor Lewis-Smith. The award-winning comedy director Geoff Posner was equally complimentary: 'Like French and Saunders, or Morecambe and Wise, it's about timing and the interplay of characters. It goes back to music hall – which was more carefully constructed and rehearsed than most audiences ever realised.'

Sitting with their directors and the rest of the team, Matt and David worked endlessly on the timing of the sketches, knowing that one glance or one gesture could make the difference between a scene that worked and one that failed. They wanted to get the pace right – to mix the longer sketches with the short, the visual with the verbal, the subtle with the outrageous. 'We have always liked the idea of those explosive comic moments that make people go: "Oh my God, can you believe it?" A bit like Hale and Pace did with the cat in the microwave,' says David.

They also like the simple one-liners. 'No pressure, but if you don't get it we'll have to sell the rabbit' are the final words of the stage mother from hell as she pushes her son to yet another drama audition, for example. Then there's the teacher who married an ex-pupil and can't see her any other way. When her parents come to visit and praise their daughter's pudding, she tells them it was a Nigella recipe. 'Nigella? You copied it from another girl?' her husband shouts, throwing the dish into the bin. The list could go on and on.

Matt and David added two less common ingredients to the *Little Britain* mix: pathos and sadness. For all the monsters in their cast list, they had their fair share of tragic figures as well. These characters would raise just as many laughs as their more strident counterparts. But their back stories and personal histories would often stick in the memory for longer.

The ever-hopeful transvestite Emily Howard is a key example. In the pilot episode the pair filmed in early 2003, her opening scene is heartbreaking and humorous in equal measure. David's Emily is buying a ticket at her local swimming pool – where, naturally, she will subsequently have to go into either the male or the female changing rooms. It is clearly a make-or-break occasion for the character and David plays her with all the nervousness, bravado and fear that a real-life event like this might arouse. There are all the distractions and desperations that a character like Emily might conjure up in a bid to live her dream. But in the end there is just hard, cold reality in front of her. Matt, impassive as the ticket-seller, isn't giving her an inch and you see how close Emily always is to public humiliation.

'It is not so much comedy, as a mini comedy drama, with the emphasis on the sad, dignified drama,' was how one critic saw those first Emily Howard scenes. 'There is a heroism to Emily Howard's desire to overcome all the obstacles life has put in front of her. There is sadness in the way she will never persuade others to see her as she sees herself. And there is tragedy in the fact that she knows this better than anyone.'

Running through each of the characters in the first series of the show could easily take a whole book in itself – there were nearly 60 of them, showing just how much work and imagination went behind the production.

But of the key players, final mention must go to Lou and Andy, the pair born out of the four-minute *Ralf Little Show* sketch spoofing Lou Reed and Andy Warhol. The premise behind the new-look Lou and Andy is that the latter is supposedly wheelchair-bound In fact, Matt's Andy is able-bodied and simply relies on David's ever-kindly Lou to do everything for him. One running joke is that Lou frequently repeats back to Andy a selection of phrases that you simply cannot imagine his monosyllabic charge ever actually saying. 'But I thought you said you hated France? I thought you said the French could never be forgiven for surrendering to the German war machine and collaborating with their occupiers to set up the Vichy government' being a classic example, prompted by Andy announcing that he now wants to go over the Channel rather than to Chessington World of Adventures as he had previously claimed.

Of course, their scenes have also given rise to a number of well-loved comedy catchphrases: 'I want that one', normally accompanied by a vague gesture at something he hasn't even looked at. And 'Yeah I know' to any suggestion from Lou. Within a matter of weeks of the first BBC2 broadcast, both lines had joined the list of the country's favourite comedic quotes. Lines from the Vicky Pollard, Emily Howard and Daffyd sketches were also starting to echo around offices, factories, classrooms and chatrooms. It was only when hopeful Conservative leader David Cameron quoted Vicky Pollard on *Newsnight*, for example, that party modernisers became convinced he had the top job in the bag. Back in London, Matt and David were finally starting to believe that they had made their breakthrough, and that after nearly a decade of struggles and professional knock-backs they had finally become the overnight sensations they had always dreamed of being.

That feeling was confirmed by the viewing figures for the BBC2 series. The 3 million who were watching might seem small beer compared to the 23 million who had watched the Christmas edition of *Only Fools and*

Horses in the pre-multi-channel world of 1996. But in 2004, 3 million was seen as an extraordinary figure for a new BBC2 sketch show. And what's more, it was the right 3 million people. 'If the only people who liked us were 20-year-old blokes I would be worried,' Matt said at the time. 'But the show has a broader appeal than that and that's because there is a lot of different comedy in it: visual jokes, satirical stuff, social observation. And there's some stuff that is pretty revolting,' he admitted, knowing how important it was to keep those original 20-year-old blokes on side.

Even in those early days, Matt says he was aware of just how diverse their audience had become. Immediately after that first series had ended its run, he took a rare holiday, in Madeira, that most old-fashioned of holiday resorts. Once there, he found several pensioners in his hotel recognised him and started quoting some of their favourite lines at him over breakfast.

Back in London, he and David spent hours on the phone to the *Little Britain* production team trying to find out how the industry was judging their shows. Most importantly, they needed to know what the BBC thought – and whether it was going to commission a second series. Days and weeks passed before a decision was made and with every unreturned phone call the men feared that they might have yet again missed their moment. *Little Britain* fever seemed to be turning into a phenomenon. But without a second series Matt and David were terrified that it could all turn cold in an instant. There is always another comedy, always another newcomer ready to take over the public consciousness, as both of them are all too aware. And they were desperate not to see *Little Britain* overtaken so soon. Fortunately, the BBC was thinking the same way. The contracts for the second series came through in the late spring – just as the show's marketing department went into overdrive.

The twin events gave Matt and David one of the busiest and most challenging years of their lives. The two men who had thought they worked as hard as almost anyone else in showbusiness were about to move up another gear. First of all, every newspaper, magazine and chat-show host wanted to interview them. Then the merchandising executives got on the case. At their request, Matt and David pulled on their Lou and Andy costumes for a nationwide tour to promote a book of the scripts from the first series. And anyone who thought no one would buy scripts in attention-deficit, blog-reading Britain was in for a surprise. Matt and David rang up 130,000 sales in less than six months – easily putting them in the *Sunday Times* hardback top ten of the year chart and pushing a large pile of royalties into their current accounts.

And it wasn't just their bank managers that they were making happy. The pair signed up to do their first full live gig in nearly five years in support of the Teenage Cancer Trust. The TCT's fundraising events are high profile and top quality – so Matt and David were determined to put on a good show. Jamie Theakston and Anthony Head were among a band of long-time supporters who also agreed to take part, and everyone got together with their original director Geoff Linehan to work on an act. On the night itself, Steve Coogan called the performers on to the Albert Hall's big stage – and the audience went wild.

In the first of four sketches, Matt and David ran through a favourite Lou and Andy scene – where Lou's 'I thought you said violence was the last bastion of moral cowardice' line sounds as unlikely as ever and comes as Andy climbs out of his chair to beat up some yobs on a park bench behind them.

Then there's Sebastian – jealous of the way new assistant Jamie Theakston is helping Anthony Head (who, as usual, is happy to have his body examined and pawed at by David's Sebastian). Vicky Pollard was up next with her six parallel baby buggies. She is studying for her 'B-Tech in *Hollyoaks*' and tells David's teacher 'Don't you give me evils' – to a roar from the crowd. Finally, of course, there was Daffyd's coming-out sketch – in which his parents display none of the shock and awe that he had been hoping for.

Matt and David both say that being able to raise money for charity is an unexpected benefit of sudden fame, as is the chance to raise the profile of good causes that might otherwise go unnoticed. Matt, for example, picked the little-known Karen Morris Memorial Trust for his share of the £125,000 he and Vic Reeves won on the *Celebrity Who Wants To Be A Millionaire* show in 2003. He became a patron of the charity shortly afterwards.

In the rush of activity after the first series of the show had been aired, both men also squeezed in a host of other jobs. Matt, for example, walked into the heartland of Middle England when he presented the annual Travel Awards for the *Daily Telegraph* at the Waldorf Hilton hotel in London – dressed as Marjorie Dawes. David, always the intellectual, used up a rare night off as a guest on *Late Review*, where he commented confidently on Tom Wolfe's novel and all the other art stories of the moment.

And then, of course, came the awards shows.

After the amazing success of series one, it seemed as if no awards show was complete without the two comedians in the audience and up on the stage. In the British Comedy Awards, hosted as usual by Jonathan Ross, it was clear that the previous year's Best Newcomer award for David had only been the start. In 2004 the boys collected three gongs, including Best TV Comedy (they beat *The Office* and *Nighty Night*). They also jointly won the Best Comedy Actor award (beating Ricky Gervais and Martin Clunes). At the National Television Awards they also won Most Popular Comedy Programme – seen as all the sweeter for having been voted for by the viewing public. Finally, as a sign that they had really made it to the heart of the performance establishment, they also picked up a Best Comedy Performance Bafta.

Coasting along on this wave of success would have been a brilliant experience for the two men. But both were aware of one small problem: the fact that they had to simultaneously write, rehearse and film the vital second series of their show. The deadline was approaching fast and expectations were high – but neither man was prepared to cut corners or rely on the goodwill of their audiences. 'Surely, when you have reached your current level of popularity it doesn't really matter what the characters do, as long as all the favourite catchphrases are there,' one journalist proclaimed during an interview in the second half of 2004. The pair were appalled at the idea and found it hard to reply. 'I think people would see through it quite quickly if that was all you did,' an angry David managed to say, when he'd calmed down enough to speak – then quickly moved to terminate the interview.

For the whole of the summer, David and Matt had been tightening up their team and working on that second series. Old mate Rob Brydon had joined them as script editor, while Matt Livesy was on board as their new director. Myfanwy Moore was still there as executive producer and most of the behind-the-scenes staff who had created the show's look, feel and sound were also raring to go.

First up, as had happened with the first series, there were some budgetary battles to fight. Perhaps surprisingly, Matt and David still didn't have the clout to win them all. So the wild Scottish hotelier Ray McCooney was largely put on ice, for example, when the £6,000 cost of his Ye Olde Hotele set was judged excessive. 'When it comes to the money it is all about compromise,' Matt admitted – appreciating that some of the extraordinary new costumes they were after for the second series (think Bubbles de Vere) would entail shelling out more than a whole episode of *Rock Profile* had cost to make five years earlier.

When the scripts were written and the filming process began, the idea had been for the show to get a prime comedy slot on BBC2. But in the BBC's White City headquarters, other people had their eye on the show as well. One of them was BBC1 Controller Lorraine Heggessey. She was a long-time fan of Matt and David. And she was determined to get their show on her channel – whatever the traditionalists might say. When the news broke that *Little Britain* was to go on the corporation's flagship channel, no one could quite believe that its comic edge could stay sharp. Surely, in the mainstream, the humour would have to be more restrained? Surely the sketches and characters would have to be edited?

Matt and David rushed to deny the charges and defend their creation. 'Any changes we have made to the show, we would have made anyway,' said Matt as they worked on the final edits. 'We were only told it was going to be on BBC1 after most of it was written. If anything it is even edgier than last time.' Insiders who had seen the preview tapes could confirm that this was indeed the case. In a while it would be obvious that the last thing Matt and David were doing was playing it safe in this make-or-break second series.

Also clear was the faith the BBC had in the show – as the start of the series approached, *Little Britain* was almost impossible to ignore. The BBC had rented billboard sites across the country to promote the new series. It got an initial screening on BBC3, where nearly 2 million viewers tuned in, smashing records for the channel and helping it earn its first ever placing in the yearly Top 20 of cable, satellite and digital TV ratings charts among the usual premium football matches on Sky Sports. But the main event was *Little Britain's* BBC1 launch.

It had a prime-time slot booked on 3 December and Matt and David took part in a media blitz of interviews and photo-shoots in the preceding weeks to keep interest sky high. And they weren't the only ones in demand. Anthony Head was back in the news and even Tom Baker got an extra job out of the show – the BBC hired him to do every continuity announcement on BBC1 for the opening night of the series (and Matt and David had been hired to write them). 'We wanted to make people sit up and notice that *Little Britain* had come to BBC1,' said Matthew Scarff, the creative producer who hired Tom for the role. As it turned out there was little danger of anyone missing it.

The series opened in typical style. 'Britain, Britain, Britain. Opened by the Queen in 1972,' boomed Tom Baker in yet another extraordinary intro. 'Britain now attracts hundreds of visitors a year. But why do they come? Not just to discover how chicken nuggets should really taste, or to take part in the great British tradition of dogging. No, they come in their droves to meet the people of Britain. And it is them what we now here look at now today. Let's rock!' First up was a Vicky Pollard sketch, in which David – as an utterly convincing supermarket security guard – watches her stuff pick and mix into her shell-suit trousers.

All the other old favourites were soon on display as well, including Lou and Andy, Daffyd, Marjorie Dawes, Sebastian and the Prime Minister and, finally, Mr Mann as the least likely dating-agency boss since Sid James in *Carry on Loving*. As usual, a vast number of individual comic lines bear repeating to show just how good this second series was. Take Daffyd, for example, who is being offered a role as a gay liaison officer in the local police force.

'We want someone who is gay who can go to the bars and clubs and talk to the gay community in their own language,' the officer tells him.

'They have their own language?' a typically horrified Daffyd replies.

What got audiences talking the next day, and got several newspapers up in arms, was a selection of new delights in the cast list (the word 'delights' is used in its loosest possible sense here). They were, said one commentator the following morning, a list of characters drawn largely from medical institutions, police courts and the autistic spectrum.

The least controversial newcomers included Matt as Florence, a cross-dressing protégé of Emily Howard. 'She has big hair and a moustache and looks exactly like David Seaman,' Matt said, having made the whole crew fall about when he first came out of make-up. Their dialogue sparkled as brightly as their dresses. 'Two ladies' tickets for the ballet, *s'il vous plaît*,' Emily asks at the opera box office before the pair started to talk about their childhoods. 'My friend always dreamed of being a prima ballerina,' says Emily.

'Yes. But then I became a hod carrier,' says Florence.

A host of old-time performers and big-name actors had also lined up to share some *Little Britain* magic. Former *Hi-De-Hi!* star Ruth Madoc was there as Daffyd's mother (sadly, Tom Jones had turned down the chance to appear as his father), while Nigel Havers had signed up to be Leader of the Opposition in the Sebastian and Michael sketches. David had another great role as Carol, the flat-haired bank clerk with the Deirdre Barlow glasses and the sudden cough. With Carol, 'Computer says no' got its first hearing and joined *Little Britain's* ever-growing catchphrase hall of fame.

The real controversy came with two other sketches. The first set to get people talking were those featuring Middle England stalwarts Maggie and Judy. The ladies happily mingled in their village, visiting friends, judging at fetes, listening to carols – but, as soon as they came into contact with anything that didn't seem white, heterosexual and British, the projectile vomiting began – including one scene in which a girl dressed as a Brownie got drenched. ('Everyone said we couldn't possibly do this to a Brownie,' says David. 'But we did. And we found the cutest one of all to get it.') Over the coming months, more problems were to arise over Maggie and Judy's apparent membership of the WI – of which more later. But in the first week of the second series, the issue was simply of bad taste.

This could hardly have been a bigger issue in the first star cameo of the series, when Vanessa Feltz played herself as the celebrity guest at a Fat Fighters group. Marjorie Dawes was, of course, unrelentingly rude to the woman she clearly saw as upstaging her. She constantly interrupts her, mistakes her for Anthea Turner and keeps reminding her of her personal problem and of how fat she was in the past. And then, it happened. At the end of the sketch, when Vanessa tries to have the last word, Matt's Marjorie spits in her face. Quite literally. Spittle drips down Vanessa's face as the Fat Fighters members (and the television audience at home) looked on, aghast. A new television taboo had been broken, though in the end no one lodged any official complaints and Vanessa herself says the sketch was one of the funniest she had ever made. 'She was very up for it,' said producer Geoff Posner of the moment that made headlines for weeks.

Having weathered the critical storm after the first few episodes of their second series had been broadcast, Matt and David were to get even more good news as 2004 drew to a close. The DVD of the show's first series was launched in October, retailing at £19.99 – and sales went through the roof. By the time Christmas arrived, more than 1.3 million copies had been sold, at a total value of nearly £26 million. The DVD was the best-selling non-film title of the year – streets ahead of the 222,000 sales of its nearest rival, *The Office Christmas Specials* DVD. At the same time, *Little Britain* also cleaned up in the audio charts – series one and two of the Radio Four shows had been released and ended up taking first and third position in the year's sales charts, separated by a new version of *The Hitchhiker's Guide to the Galaxy*.

It seemed that viewers couldn't get enough of the shows. As well as a double episode of *EastEnders*, BBC3 controller Stuart Murphy had decided to fill his Christmas Day evening schedule with a wall-to-wall, six-hour block of *Little Britain* – a show he described as '*The Two Ronnies* on acid'. As none of the *Little Britain* shows was new, and more than a million copies of the first series had just been sold on DVD, it was a big gamble to assume that enough other people would still be interested in the show. But Murphy was right, and won his channel its biggest ever audience share, coming second only to BBC1 and ITV in the big day's ratings battle. Not even a specially recorded Christmas message to Britain from *The Simpsons* could compete with Matt and David's creations – they beat Channel Four's viewing totals by more than 100,000 and left BBC2 and Channel Five equally far adrift. It was the day the BBC's digital channels finally made it into the big league and the broadcasting establishment said it owed the *Little Britain* creators a huge debt.

Famous supporters were also lining up to praise the show that Christmas. Johnny Depp said he wanted a bit part in a sketch; Cherie Blair said it was required viewing at No. 10. As far as royal seal of approval went, the pair had all their bases covered. First of all, Prince Charles's spokesman said he and Camilla loved the sketches, which he felt reflected the heritage of his favourite *Goons* sketches from the 1950s; and Princes Harry and William simply loved it, full stop.

With so much going for them, Matt and David could be excused for wanting to relax and let their guard down over Christmas and New Year. They had finally made the leap into the entertainment A-list – and they were doing it on their own terms and in their own way. They hadn't compromised their characters and they were loving every minute of their newfound success. Toasting the start of 2005, they couldn't have been more optimistic about their futures. Unfortunately, they were both about to get the shock of their lives.

CHAPTER 13

THE BACKLASH

When it came, the turning of the tide against *Little Britain* was both fast and furious. Academic and author Felipe Fernandez-Armesto was one of the first to attack Matt and David for allegedly thinking it is 'cool to be cruel'. He wrote that the show 'ridicules the handicapped, homosexuals, you name it' and was in danger of destroying the country's entire comic heritage. 'There is good bad taste and bad bad taste and the British – though once paramount in the art – no longer seem to know the difference. Great Britain is becoming Gross Britain,' he wrote in an article that was syndicated to papers across the country.

Another writer, Barbara Ellen in the *Observer*, was even tougher. Her criticism was measured and well thought out. And it hit some pretty raw nerves. 'Am I the only one heartily sick of *Little Britain*, in particular their teen mum grotesque Vicky Pollard?' she began, as the second series drew to a close. 'It seems to me that too much of

221

their comedy is ill-conceived and spiteful and mainly aimed at the working class in a self-satisfied chattering-class manner that makes you want to thump them really hard. Watching *Little Britain*, you come away with this slimy feeling, as if you have been watching a fox hunt, only in this case the animals being torn apart are the poorest, most helpless members of our society.'

And Ellen felt there was more wrong with *Little Britain* than just the Vicky Pollard character. Misogyny, cruelty, indifference, careless callousness, she ran through it all and summed the show up as: 'Sloppy, hit and miss comedy writing. Endless "fat" jokes, "gay" jokes, "thick" jokes, "bodily fluid" jokes and a new female character again (tee hee!) grotesquely fat, running around naked with her pendulous tits swinging and pubic hair showing.'

What made Ellen's comments even harder for Matt and David to bear was the fact that she then compared them – very unfavourably – with all the comic heroes they had spent a lifetime trying to emulate. This was particularly evident in what she saw as the class war in their writing. 'Look at the work of your elders and betters,' she advised. 'When the gifted Les Dawson dressed up as an "old biddy" gossiping in a pinny over the garden fence he did it with affection, not spite. Similarly, when the likes of Peter Kay, Johnny Vegas, Caroline Aherne and Craig Cash portray their backgrounds they don't wade in like school bullies, pointing and sniggering at the "freaks". Having actually "lived it" they have a genuine tenderness for their subjects, a perfect understanding of the delicate nuances, the essential pathos and triumphs of working-class life. They give the people they depict a dignity which is completely absent from equivalent character sketches in *Little Britain.*'

As her final shot, she took direct aim at the home-counties boys who had written the comedy hit of the day. 'It could just be that I have a lifelong aversion to middle-class people making money by sneering at the "funny little ways" of working-class people, whose lives they know, and care, nothing about.'

Of course, in reality Matt and David could hardly be described as simply waging a war on the working classes – not least because they were simultaneously in trouble with the official representatives of Britain's middle classes.

At issue here was the image of the Women's Institute – in the form of the second-series stalwarts Maggie and Judy. 'No more lesbian jam – I can't keep it down' was just one of their best lines as they projectile-vomited after hearing that food was made from a same-sex couple – or from an Ainsley Harriott recipe, or if anything else upset their Middle England sensibilities. The inspiration for the characters had come from a documentary made back in 1999 by photographer Martin Parr, the man who had inspired much of the original look of *Little Britain.* That show, *Modern Times: Think of England*, had seen Parr take a look at what made Britain British – and the scenes of the women who ruled their local fetes with a rod of iron had long since stuck in Matt and David's minds.

The problem was that in several of the early sketches

the pair were seen in front of the distinctive lettering and logo of the Women's Institute – and, quite understandably, a legal letter was subsequently sent to the BBC, pointing out that the connection between the bigoted ladies and the real-life WI was unfair. 'We love a laugh and a joke like everyone else but this was a little bit extreme,' said Fran Saltmarsh, vice-chairman of the National Federation of Women's Institutes. 'We have always been an organisation for every woman, whatever her social standing, race, creed or nationality. Whoever wishes to join can do so.' The WI's honorary treasurer Sally Roberts was among a huge group of members who agreed that they found *Little Britain* funny – but she too said they had to draw the line at the inference that the members were homophobic or racist. 'The implications in this sketch on such a popular BBC show are damaging and hurtful to our members,' she stated.

Matt, David and the top brass at the BBC agreed straight away that they had gone too far. 'It was never our intention to cause offence or upset to members of the WI,' said the BBC's official statement. And with Matt and David's blessing the institute's logo was wiped out of the previously filmed scenes and would not appear in any new ones.

The episode showed that, despite their very public bravado, the pair were actually very careful about which boundaries they crossed, and which they avoided. 'Some things are not appropriate for BBC1,' David admitted, when asked about the editing of some of the more extreme sketches after the digital to mainstream jump was first mooted. Some of the scenes of him suckling at the breast of his screen mother Geraldine James were a case in point, while a host of other images were also deemed inappropriate for a terrestrial audience.

'In the second series there were a load of sketches about a mother and daughter who run a motorway service station. They always end up having sex with a trucker behind the café by the bins. After watching them we felt this was possibly a step too far for TV. We didn't think people were quite ready to see me getting rogered up against some bins,' admitted David.

'Our parents watch, so we have to be good,' added Matt, saying the pair also self-edited the final scene to the 'Jason and Nan' storyline, which they had planned to use at the end of the second series. In it, David as Jason and former *Grange Hill* actress Evie Garrett as Nan go far further than the infamous toe-sucking scene (Evie wrongly thought David might find the experience more comfortable if she put strong-scented body lotion on her toes before he started licking them — he didn't). 'In the end we realised that the final scene was very naughty, a bit too extreme, even for us,' David said, before admitting it would probably end up on the DVD release (which it did, alongside a host of other deleted scenes and out-takes).

Interestingly enough, the different personalities of the two men often come into sharpest focus when their work is under fire – as it was in the early days of 2005, when their second series was being shown. Matt, always happier in the background, tends to take the view that the less they say the sooner any storm will pass. He feels the work should stand or fall on its own merits and be judged accordingly. Furious about the criticism, David, however, prefers to come out fighting. When any aspects of the show need defending, he is the man to do it. Accusations of 'class tourism' – the pair's supposed attacks on the working class through figures such as Vicky Pollard – trigger a typical rebuttal: 'Vicky is not a victim or a statistic. She responds to events on her own terms, and people like her. OK, they might not want to marry her or have her living next door but she is a very "up" character. She's a winner, not a victim.

'It is the same with Daffyd His character is fun. You want to spend time with him. You don't despise him and you laugh with and not at him. And don't forget our characters represent all social backgrounds. We celebrate difference and we don't regard any of our characters with contempt. We love them all,' David insisted. His words tumbled out – he clearly felt rattled at having to defend and protect his comedy creations.

Of course, what the men soon realised was that very little they could do or say would appease their fiercest critics – especially as in many cases they couldn't do right for doing wrong. At the same time that they were being attacked for supposedly being cruel to single mothers in the Vicky Pollard sketches, they were also being criticised for 'glamorising anti-social behaviour' in the very same scenes. To add to the confusion, writer

Craig Brown even nominated Vicky as a 'People's Peer' on Radio Four in recognition of her achievements as an icon of modern Britain.

After a while, and after talking it all through with colleagues and their families, Matt and David realised that the best thing to do was to just let the storms crash over them. They knew their comedy was intended to be kind rather than cruel, so they were prepared to simply shake off anyone who challenged them on that front. But, while that was ultimately quite easy to do, another challenge proved somewhat harder. The pair also had to face up to the more fundamental question of whether their second series was, at the end of the day, any good.

A small but growing band of critics seemed ready to talk down the show they had spent the past year talking up. The writers were attacked as being capable only of 'catchphrase comedy' that had already started to run out of steam. '*Little Britain* essentially survives, just as *The Fast Show* did, by playing out endless variations of the same basic gags,' a viewer wrote on one 'fan' website. Worse, a small but growing band of voices were now saying that the boys' lovingly created characters were already turning into caricatures, the suggestion being that they had no depth, and no real life beyond the confines of their sketches.

Equally depressing was a revival of the criticism that the show was just a rehash of ideas, themes and styles from the likes of *The League of Gentlemen* and *The Fast Show*. Critics said Fat Fighters leader Marjorie Dawes was a direct copy from Royston Vasey and the work-restart officer Pauline, and that Vicky Pollard could have come direct from *The Fast Show*.

'We can ignore that because it has always been like this,' says David. 'I am sure that when *The Office* first came along everyone said it was just like *People Like Us*. Everyone is always being compared to someone and as long as you are compared to good people I don't think it matters.' More importantly, David argues that, far from being derivative and safe, he and Matt had been defying conventional wisdom when they drew the templates for *Little Britain*. 'I think we are original, not least because when we said we wanted to do a show in front of an audience with a laughter track people thought we were mad, because that wasn't the kind of show being done. It wasn't the kind of thing winning awards or getting critical acclaim. But we did it anyway.'

According to some people, they shouldn't have bothered, though. The *Mail on Sunday*'s normally ebullient television critic Jaci Stephen was reluctantly negative when she wrote about the show that winter. 'Comics always expect a backlash when they follow up a hugely successful first series, and they usually blame the critics for doing that British thing of building people up, only to knock them down,' she observed. 'Well, it gives me no pleasure to say this, but the first episode of the second series was a massive disappointment. I loved the first series, so much so that I reviewed it nearly every week, and I would have loved nothing more than to say that this series is every bit as good.

'But what has happened? What was a brilliant theatre of characters, all of whom came to you, so it seemed, with a dark history, have turned into infantile grotesques, who spit, vomit and say "p★★★". The subtlety has gone, and although some of the favourites remain they have lost their edge. The Prime Minister's sidekick, Sebastian, is now a pantomime character; Fat Fighters' Marjorie Dawes is no longer spiteful but gruesome; only Daffyd, Lou and Andy have held on to their original charm.'

And Jaci, sounding genuinely upset about the way she saw the show going, wasn't finished. 'Is this what happens when you are told you are going to BBC1?' she asked. 'Ditch the charm in favour of schoolboy smut and stomach-churning hideousness? BBC3 is a breeding ground for talent and Matt Lucas and David Walliams have it by the bucket load. But they have turned the genius of their first series into a mere sketch show with not very good punchlines and it's heartbreaking.'

As a pair of perfectionists who see attacks on their characters and their comedy as attacks on their integrity, this kind of criticism was hard to bear for the duo. And they were about to get involved in yet another argument – over how often their programmes were being broadcast. The mass showing of the two series on BBC3 at Christmas had been seen as a triumph at the time. But did it hide a more worrying trend?

Episodes of *Little Britain* had been repeated an astonishing 175 times in 2004 – making it the most repeated show ever in a 12-month period (the previous record had been for 125 repeats in 2003 – also of *Little Britain*). Over the course of the year, the broadcasting analysts calculated that each of the 14 *Little Britain* episodes had been broadcast at least 12 times – with the programme shown 54 times in December alone. And this was at a time when BBC boss Mark Thompson had pledged to cut repeats across the whole BBC network. 'We are in danger of killing the goose that laid the golden egg,' said a BBC spokesman, amid concerns that the saturation coverage might cause viewers to tire of the show before the following year's third series had even been filmed.

So what could Matt and David do to try and turn this situation around? As it turned out, they didn't have time to do anything, because they had already committed themselves to a quite different project. One that would put all their success, and all the critics, in perspective. They were going to Africa with Comic Relief. And they were in for one of the most shattering experiences of their lives.

In early 2005, the pair got on the plane to the Ethiopian capital of Addis Ababa. It was a place halfway across the world where no one knew their names, let alone their characters and the controversy that was building up around them. And Addis Ababa is somewhere both men say they will never forget. David, who says he never knew poverty existed in Britain until he was an adult, and had never been in a council block until his twenties, was particularly hard hit by the scenes they saw in Africa.

On the first morning of their visit, Matt and David headed out with a handful of workers and volunteers from the Irish charity Goal, which helps set up shelters for street children, shelters that are desperately needed every day. 'We saw thousands of destitute people, limbs missing, skin diseased...' Matt tails off into silence at the memory. And what happened next was even more shocking. As ever, when Westerners are seen, the group and their guides were surrounded by desperate locals, begging for anything they could eat, use or sell. 'One of our group gave a desperate boy some money and he was immediately jumped upon by a swarm of his elders, and the money was gone. It is an intensely intimidating atmosphere,' Matt admitted afterwards.

What both men noticed straight away was the effect that AIDS has had on the country. The disease has wiped out almost an entire generation of Ethiopians, just as it has done over much of Africa. 'Walk around the streets, the slums, the projects and it is eerie as hell. You will see children and old folk, but no one of our age. They died,' says Matt who had already confessed that the African visit had been a big hurdle for him. 'I had developed a weary tolerance to even the most alarming footage,' he said. 'I was more likely to shed a tear watching *EastEnders* than on being reminded of the appalling statistic that every three seconds a child dies of hunger and preventable diseases – that's more than 30,000 children a day. It's understandable, really, because what is happening out there is so unbelievably shocking, so utterly wrong, that we daren't even think about it. So you can appreciate that, although I didn't say it out loud to many people, I really didn't want to go.'

Having faced his demons, Matt was the first to say that if you look hard enough you can find positive action in Africa – such as the uplifting work that Goal did, for both boys and girls, for example. And other Comic Relief-funded operations that they toured and watched in action that spring were starting to show results, even though everything was just a small drop in a huge and ugly ocean of misery.

As they flew back to London, both Matt and David agreed that they needed to do more to help. So Matt decided to write an open letter to the *Sun* to detail the highs and lows of the visit and to encourage as many others as possible to contribute to the relief effort. 'I have never been an activist. I am a comedian, not a politician,' he wrote. 'I never thought I would be writing a piece like this. The thing is, you cannot go and see what I have seen and just walk away. Indifference is no longer an option. I know what is happening. I am now responsible, and by reading this so are you. We cannot close our eyes to this degree of suffering any more. We just cannot. Please, please, do anything you can to help.'

A week after arriving back in Britain, Matt and David were still trying to shake off the depression that had engulfed them since first arriving in Africa. It wasn't easy, not least because it seemed as if the criticism about their work had continued apace while they had been away. It seemed at times like far more than just a typical game of building people up to knock them down. Sometimes it got personal – as if a handful of journalists not only thought the duo's show was nosediving, but also actively disliked them as people.

Unsure of what to do, the pair decided to put everything into a post-Africa perspective. Then they would fight back in the most obvious way available to them – by working harder than ever and by trying to raise a record amount of money for charity. And if in the process they could prove that as far as their careers were concerned the best was yet to come, then all the better.

The new stage on which they felt they could prove themselves was the biggest in the comedy and the charity year. Comic Relief had been launched on Christmas Day in 1985 with a live broadcast from a refugee camp in Sudan. The aim had been to wake viewers up about the horrors that were happening on the other side of the world and to raise money to try and put things right. The fundraising activities gradually became more sophisticated over the next couple of years. The first Red Nose Day took place in 1998. The broadcast was hosted by Lenny Henry, Griff Rhys Jones and Jonathan Ross and raised £15 million – an amount that would soon be dwarfed as the entertainment community offered its wholehearted support to the project. To date it has raised some £360 million. Matt and David had both taken part in several previous Red Nose Day events in their various comedy incarnations –

and had even helped behind the scenes when they were just another unknown act on the comedy circuit. In 2005, however, they had the chance to make a really big contribution. And with a little bit of help from some new and famous friends they swore they would confound their critics with their strongest and most honest performances yet.

Robbie Williams was the first star the men wanted to get on board. And he accepted on the spot. Robbie had been a fan of their work since their *Rock Profile* days, when he had learned many of their sketches off by heart. Since then he had become a good friend. So he was prepared to do anything to help – which, in this instance, included wandering into the new ladies dress shop that had been set up by Matt and David's Emily and Florence, quipping that he had thought he was in Mister Byrite. It was a small step from there to getting the pop star into the onscreen dressing room, out of his jeans and (behind the screen) out of his thong and into an Edwardian dress. 'I'm a lady!' Robbie cried as he dashed out of the shop, parasol in hand and a pink rose in his hair. The sketch was recorded in a studio and on location, ready to be played on Red Nose Day itself.

Most of the other acts that Matt and David were planning were a little different. They were going to be recorded in front of a live audience, so everyone knew they had to be good. The first would test George Michael's sense of humour – not least because he was going to be referred to as 'George Michaels' throughout a Lou and Andy sketch in which Lou presents him as a surprise guest at Andy's birthday dinner. Having said he wanted to meet the star, Andy, of course, changes his mind when 'Mr Michaels' actually appears. 'I don't like him. I want him to go. I prefer Tony Hadley,' the black-clad singer is told, before being informed that, apart from 'Jesus to a Child', Andy finds his work 'emotionally vapid'. He makes a swift exit.

Elton John was also on the pair's hit list for Comic Relief, five years after they had parodied him as an obsessive prima donna in *Rock Profile*. He too signed up straight away – agreeing to sit in on a spoof interview from an 'out of the village' Daffyd Thomas. Supposedly intent on interviewing the star for an article for the *Llanddewi Breffi Gazette*, Daffyd is on top form. 'I've often seen you around and about with this chap David Furness. Is he one of your nephews?' he asks, as Elton (who hadn't been given a script) started to laugh. Each of the next questions was full of double entendres – most of which Elton was able to match with off-the-cuff responses of his own. 'Do you let the manager make the decisions or would you come down and pull someone off at half-time?' Daffyd asks, with mock innocence, regarding the inner workings of Watford Football Club.

'If only. No I would never interfere with the manager,' Elton replies, just before being confronted with the arrival of David as a furiously camp Spanish waiter.

Matt and David also filmed a *Tricia* special, in which

Vicky Pollard came on the show, supposedly to meet her real father – plus a Sebastian sketch with Anthony Head, a Judy and Maggie sketch where a Boy Scout bore the brunt of the vomit machine and a 'Computer says no' sketch. Throw in a couple of other scenes, including a new Dennis Waterman sketch, and *Little Britain's* Comic Relief package was about as strong as it could be.

And that was important, because on the 2005 charity bill it was competing for attention with a comic version of *University Challenge* starring the likes of Hugh Grant, Stephen Fry, Neil Morrissey and *Cold Feet's* John Thomson, plus a *Spider-man* spoof staring Rowan Atkinson as Spider Plant Man who attempts to save the world and woo Rachel Stevens. Throw in contributions from comedy stalwarts such as Peter Kay, Graham Norton, Ricky Gervais, Lenny Henry and Dawn French in a special edition of *The Vicar of Dibley* and the competition for laughs was tough.

As it turned out, the *Little Britain* sketches seemed to get the critics' votes as the most successful of the evening. But when it came to raising money the real effect would be felt over the next few months. Matt and David had already edited and repackaged the scenes for a special DVD – it had topped the new release charts even before Red Nose Day arrived, selling more than 110,000 copies at HMV in four days alone. High demand kept the DVD in the best-seller charts for the next five weeks – with £3.40 from each copy sold going direct to Comic Relief.

It had been, Matt and David were pleased to reflect, a

fun job done well. And in 2005, after the Christmas 2004 tsunami had ripped through South East Asia, they were ready to help other charities as well. One simple but effective task was to autograph a road sign for Llanddewi-Brefi, the tiny Welsh hamlet that was subtly misspelled as Llanddewi Breffi in *Little Britain* and chosen as Daffyd's home town. Even though Daffyd's 'only gay in the village' scenes were actually filmed just outside Henley in Oxfordshire, the real-life Llanddewi-Brefi had become so famous that its road signs were being stolen at a rate of one a month in late 2004. It was hoped that, by creating an official, signed version, the thefts might stop. Anthony Roberts of Zodiac Signs in Merthyr Tydfil had already agreed to replace the stolen signs for free, because he is such a fan of the show, while local councillor Dai Evans arranged the charity sale of the autographed version. Dai and other local residents (the village's population numbers around 500) had already seen the show as a mixed blessing. It did bring some sporadic extra money to the area – not least when dozens of students from nearby Lampeter University descended upon it dressed as Daffyd in various fundraising stunts. Local shops were also ringing up healthy sales for unofficial T-shirts carrying the 'Nid Daffyd yw'r unig hoyw yn Llanddewi-Brefi' (for anyone whose Welsh is a little rusty it translates as: Daffyd isn't the only gay in Llanddewi-Brefi). On the down side, residents admitted that they had soon tired of journalists from London, and even abroad, knocking on doors to see if they could find any real-life Daffyds to illustrate their stories. As it turned out, the specially autographed road sign didn't actually stop the demand for local souvenirs. As the third series of the show was being broadcast the following year, two men were arrested trying to unscrew one of Zodiac's new signs.

At home in London, with Comic Relief and their other charity work out of the way, Matt and David found they were still on winning form. First of all they were voted 'the most powerful people in British comedy', toppling Graham Norton from the top slot in a poll of industry insiders. Then, the line 'I'm the only gay in the village' was voted best comedy catchphrase of all time in a survey masterminded by UKTV Gold. Tommy Cooper's 'Just like that' came second in the poll, followed by Homer Simpson's 'Doh!' and Del Boy's 'Lovely jubbly'. 'I don't believe it' from *One Foot In The Grave*, 'Here's another fine mess you got me into' from Oliver Hardy and 'Yeah baby!' from Austin Powers were joined in the second half of the top ten by Vicky Pollard's 'Yeah but no, but yeah' and Emily Howard's 'I'm a laydee' – making Matt and David the most successful writers in the chart.

In yet another comedy poll that spring, the characters Lou and Andy edged ahead of the *Monty Python* dead-parrot sketch to make No 1 in the Top 50 comedy sketches of all time, according to a Channel Four report (Vicky Pollard also made the Top 5). What made this achievement even more significant was that modern comedy had just been roundly beaten by old-time equivalents in a far broader investigation by the BBC. Its researchers and pollsters found that the 1970s were regarded as the golden age of British comedy by the general public, who rated shows such as *Fawlty Towers*, *Dad's Army*, *The Two Ronnies* and *Morecambe and Wise* far more highly than contemporary TV comedy. The 1980s were almost as popular, with shows such as *Spitting Image* and *Blackadder* seen as all-time classics. The current decade, *Little Britain*'s decade, was seen as the weakest in living memory – so the pair were overjoyed that their sketches were seen to have risen above the dross to catch the judging panel's eye.

Two final pieces of good news for the boys came in the spring – at the annual Bafta awards and the international Rose d'Or television festival in Lucerne, Switzerland. At the former, the pair collected two more statuettes – for Best Comedy Performance and Best Comedy Programme or Series, a double success that put them on a par with Ricky Gervais's *The Office*. David, however, felt the pair still had mountains left to climb as they left the ceremony at the Theatre Royal, Drury Lane. 'What I really want to win is Best Actress Award,' he said, referring to the trademark cross-dressing in *Little Britain*. It was a throwaway line. But bookies immediately reported a flurry of bets suggesting that at least a handful of people believed that David would one day achieve his goal.

Meanwhile, in Switzerland, the international awards body at the Rose d'Or gave Matt and David even more silverware for their trophy cabinets. They won Best Comedy and Best Comedy Performance – and led a great night for British talent, with other commendations going to Peter Kay, Zoë Wanamaker, Pippa Haywood and Julia Davis's extraordinary *Nighty Night*.

So was it all plain sailing for Matt and David in the awards season? Unfortunately not, as they had found out at that year's Baftas. The awards ceremony had been at its glittering best until Matt and David headed on stage to collect the first of the two Baftas they were awarded that year. But one man in the audience, *Women in Love* and *Tommy* director Ken Russell, wasn't happy. He couldn't forget the infamous scene from *Little Britain's* second series, in which Matt had spat at Vanessa Feltz. And he was ready to make his feelings known. 'Get off. You will not get a third series. You can't go spitting in people's faces,' he heckled as they headed towards the stage, though his criticism was soon drowned out by the applause of almost everyone else at the event. Afterwards, the men agreed that they would have to take the comments in their stride. 'It was odd to have incurred that kind of wrath,' said a bemused David at the after-show party. 'But actually it is rather an achievement to have offended someone like Ken Russell, isn't it? I suppose you have to take that as a great honour.'

And, anyway, shortly afterwards some other great men in their field were lining up to add to – rather than attack – the *Little Britain* mystique. Legendary photographer Mario Testino, the man who had taken the final photographs of Princess Diana and who has since immortalised almost every A-list celebrity in Hollywood, was one of them. He had watched *Little Britain* when it was broadcast in his native Brazil – and he was over the moon when *Vogue* editor Alexandra Shulman rang him up and said she wanted him to photograph the show's stars for a special issue of the fashion bible. 'The notion of pairing the glamour of Mario's photographs with the harsh comedy of *Little Britain* was irresistible. Right from the start I was sure that we needed to have a model in the pictures to contrast the *Little Britain* characters and the traditional *Vogue* world. Erin O'Connor, who is a great actress, was perfect,' said Shulman of the set-up that she created for the shoot.

David was thrilled at the idea from the start, because he was a huge fan of Testino's work and was becoming a keen collector of contemporary photography. Matt says he needed more persuading, claiming – perhaps disingenuously – that he wasn't entirely sure who the photographer was.

The plan was to create a 13-page spread of photographs for the July issue of the magazine – and, for the first shoot, everyone headed out to a west London community centre where Matt and David dressed up as Vicky Pollard and her mates. From the start, everyone agreed they were in for a masterclass in how well the men bring their characters alive and how easily they can ad-lib as them when the costumes are on.

'Yeah but, no but, yeah but, shurr'up, Testino. Is that

camera from Boots, yeah? You know you can get three for one from Boots, yeah?' was Vicky's take on the photographer. And supermodel of the moment Erin O'Connor got equally short shrift from her rival. 'Pink is so tacky. This whole thing is, like, so tacky,' a gum-chewing Vicky concluded as she watched the professional put on her flawless make-up. It was the same when Marjorie Dawes appeared for a different set of photos – she glowered from the background as the six-foot-one, rake-thin Erin stood on a pair of scales. In the final set of shots, Andy appeared – and, of course, was entirely unimpressed by the whole occasion. 'I don't want Testino. I want David Bailey,' he whined constantly as Mario's camera clicked away.

Taking on jobs like these were something of a gamble for the men as *Little Britain* fever continued to build up. Removing their biggest characters from the confines of a television sketch was good fun and turned out to act as an incredible release for them. But it also gave the impression that their simple sketch show was turning into a fully fledged industry. And as the jobs piled up, its creators were starting to wonder whether or not they could cope. 'It's like driving a car when the brakes have gone,' is the way David famously described it at the time. 'You're still steering, but you're not in control any more. The programme's not ours, now. Once your inventions are being quoted in schools and offices they have a life of their own, independent of anything you might do or say.' In a bizarre kind of way, David even admitted that some

242

of the individual characters were taking control of their creators. When he met Tony Blair at a charity function, he said he subconsciously found himself lapsing into Sebastian mode and beginning to flirt with the real-life Prime Minister. But he is too discreet to say if he thought Tony noticed.

Behind the scenes, others were putting out feelers to see if the *Little Britain* effect could go global. Series producer Geoff Posner let slip that the search was on for a possible 'Only gay in Houston' as part of a transatlantic transfer. 'We have had offers from the States to sell the show as a format and they would then adapt the sketches for their audience.' But, while Matt had been told how popular the original show was on BBC America, the track record of other British shows suggested that wider audiences could be harder to attract. The American version of *The Office*, for example, had attracted a decent 11 million audience in its opening week and then saw ratings slump to just six million as US viewers struggled with its naturalistic and downbeat settings.

But if the show didn't crack American television, could its creators become the toast of Hollywood? David Thompson, Head of BBC Films, was determined to find out. He told an audience at the Cannes Film Festival that he wanted the company to branch out from its traditional range of hard-hitting subjects – which had recently included both genocide in Rwanda and the problems of young criminals in the East End of London. 'We are really trying to up the ante on comic films. The bulk of films made are dramas, but the films that audiences want to see are not. Lucas and Walliams are brilliantly inventive comedians. We've tried to get them and they are thinking about it.'

Unfortunately for Thompson (and potential cinema audiences), Matt and David had plenty of other things to think about in 2005. The first and most pressing challenge was the writing and filming of their third television series, which had already been allocated a flagship BBC1 slot in the autumn schedules. Then there was the small matter of the near-simultaneous national tour in front of an estimated 200,000 fans.

Another huge live audience was also waiting at Live 8 in London's Hyde Park – and on television and computer screens around the world. Bob Geldof's bid to 'make poverty history' while world leaders met in Gleneagles, Scotland, was a typically star-studded affair – and Matt and David, as Lou and Andy, were on stage after a Coldplay set to introduce Elton John.

These three major tasks would have been a challenge for anyone, at any time. But they presented extra problems for Matt and David in the summer of 2005. Because, after so many years of focusing entirely on their careers, both men had decided they wanted the freedom of a normal personal life as well. With the money from *Little Britain* finally starting to roll in, they were both able to live out some of their dreams – and, in the process, some key differences in their temperaments and personalities started to emerge. Matt

and David had been best friends for years, they spent the
largest part of almost every day together and they had a
huge amount in common. But they were also very
different people. And, in the summer of 2005, it
suddenly seemed as if they might be going in very
different directions.

CHAPTER 14

PRIVATE LIVES

'Mum, I'm gay.' In the iconic Daffyd Thomas sketch, the big revelation is met with almost total indifference. Daffyd's mother carries on with the ironing (which includes her son's studded leather belt) while his dad carries on reading his paper. 'Oh, that's nice, dear,' says Ruth Madoc as his mum. 'Yeah, good for you, lad,' says his dad, going back to an article about a stolen bucket. The scene paved the way for a stream of jokes about the other vast number of other gays in Daffyd's village, and indeed in his family. And the sketch would become one of the favourites on the live tour and in *Little Britain* 'best-of' polls.

The first time Matt Lucas used the phrase 'Mum, I'm gay' wasn't in a radio, television or theatre sketch, however. It was in real life, in his early twenties, when he decided to tell his mother about his sexuality. And, in real life, reactions are rarely what you might expect. Diana Lucas didn't respond to the news with the casual

247

equanimity of a comedy character. And, while she soon accepted her son's situation, and has been a close friend and confidante to him ever since, she was initially shocked at his revelation.

Matt says that, after talking things through and reassuring Diana, his next challenge was to tell David – and protect their professional partnership. 'After I came out to my mum, I was feeling a bit wobbly and shaky and I rang David up and said he would have to bear with me for a few days.'

David, who had long since guessed his friend was gay and had been waiting for the subject to come out into the open, said he could take as long as he needed. Though he couldn't really see what all the fuss was about. 'Who has ever been surprised by somebody coming out?' he asks. 'It just doesn't surprise people. Maybe if your dad comes out it's different. But with friends and family? Come on. Everyone knows.' And, as far as David was concerned, nobody cared, which was just how it should be.

Of course, this easy acceptance in itself created issues that had to be dealt with – laying the foundation blocks for the whole set of Daffyd sketches. 'I identify with the idea of growing up and not being confident about your sexuality, or knowing about it and not feeling that you can talk about it with people,' says Matt. 'Then you finally come out and go through that awful sense of anti-climax. Which is probably a very common experience. As a gay person, you mythologise yourself. You create yourself as this hero in your own life and then you come out and it's slightly disappointing. It doesn't suddenly make everything right and you don't feel special any more. I can remember coming out to one friend and he just said, "Oh, that's cool, my girlfriend's bisexual." With other friends I did feel a bit annoyed because it didn't cause any hoo-ha and there was a complete lack of drama. It was like training for a marathon, running it, then finding out that none of your friends bothered to watch you and didn't care whether you finished or not.'

As it turned out, Matt was dealing with a few extra issues in the early days of being 'an out gayer', as Daffyd would one day say. 'I had basically accepted to myself that I was gay,' he says. 'But then a really weird thing happened. Exactly around that time I started to find women attractive. I don't know what the hell was going on there.' But it certainly added to his confusion.

Knowing that his family and friends would stick by him regardless of his sexuality was a powerful confidence booster, however. Coming out had been both a personal and a professional milestone in Matt's life. It gave him a sense of freedom and it allowed him to focus full-time on his career.

In a strange kind of way, it also allowed David to talk more about the sexually ambiguous comedy characters he had been creating in his head for years. Having proved that he was happy to have a gay best friend, he felt he was able to laugh at the gay community with impunity. Daffyd was one of the few characters the pair have created that was born more from one of the duo – David – than the other. Having always known that the announcement from Matt would come one day, he had sketched out a range of scenarios for it in his head. As another of their friends came out, to no great surprise, the comic creating continued. By the time Matt told David that he *had* to watch the Brian Dowling dynamic unfolding on *Big Brother*, the whole Daffyd character was already pretty much formed. Now it only took Matt pulling on those red rubber shorts and extraordinary T-shirts to bring Daffyd to life.

'When you grow up gay, you can identify yourself by your struggle to deal with it and to come out and be accepted. When that struggle is over you think, What do I do now? That's very much where David saw Daffyd,' says Matt. 'Being gay might have been the only thing you feel defined you to yourself as special and different. And, when it is revealed and doesn't make anyone bat an eyelid, you have to find something else. You have to go and find yourself a personality. That, again, is where we decided to put Daffyd, and we both felt there was a lot of mileage in seeing him try to make that leap.'

For his part, once Matt had got over the issue of telling his family and friends that he was gay, the subject was pretty much dropped. It was part of him, but it wasn't all of him, as he said when pressed about it in interviews. When pushed, he would speak to gay magazines such as *Attitude* (though always with David at his side and always to promote their work). But he didn't march, campaign or feel any need to politicise his sexuality. For many years he also didn't have any serious partners – putting that down to the standard entertainment excuse of being 'too busy' to meet anyone. But, as his career rose and fell in the 1990s, he began to admit that actually he was always looking for someone to share the highs and lows with. Someone who could enjoy the excitement of winning a commission and making it on to television. Someone to say it would all still work out when a bad review came in, or a pilot episode ended up being shelved. Friends often tried to set him up with suitable partners, even though he said blind dates were among the most terrifying events in his life. So it couldn't have felt better when it finally happened: in 2002, he met the man he wanted to fall in love, and settle down, with.

The man in question is Kevin McGee, a television producer who had been part of the Comic Relief production team, though it wasn't as part of that project that the pair met. Two years younger than Matt, he made it clear that he wanted to stay firmly out of the public eye. Matt agreed. In one rare comment about his partner, he said he had given Kevin the nickname 'Baby Bedingfield' after he had grown a beard and started to look like the pop star Daniel. But beyond this, Matt agreed that they should keep their relationship as private as possible. He said the pair enjoyed a life of 'reclusive domesticity', they have rarely been photographed together and avoid London's celebrity circuit like the plague. Friends say that a less likely couple to invite the likes of *Hello!* magazine into their 'beautiful home' would be harder to find.

Having said that, Kevin does, of course, accompany Matt to some of the biggest awards ceremonies, though he tends to stick to the background, often walking up the red carpets with Matt, but then fading away as the inevitable pre-show interviews begin. The one time Kevin did cause more of a stir was at Matt's 30th birthday party in 2004. Kevin, then 28, had arranged a bash in which as many people as possible came dressed as characters from *Hi-De-Hi!* – Matt was a star as chalet maid Peggy and the event was a brilliant success.

The following year, by which time *Little Britain* had long since transformed Matt's fortunes, the couple were able to afford a far bigger house. They moved from the student and 'young professionals' paradise of West Hampstead to a three-bedroom three-storey mews house just off the trendy Rosslyn Hill area of Hampstead. It was entertainment and luvvie paradise – near neighbours included Jamie Oliver, Jude Law and Rachel Stevens. Matt and Kevin could hardly believe they had made it to the property A-list, though they still head back to West Hampstead to catch up with old friends in their former watering holes on a regular basis. They had not yet fulfilled Matt's long-held ambition of having a genuine Mr Whippy machine in his kitchen – though that step, perhaps, is still just a matter of time.

As their anniversaries as a couple stacked up, the pair exchanged matching eternity rings – though, again, there was no Elton John and David Furnish-style flourish, let alone a civil partnership ceremony. It was simply a happy relaxed relationship. And David is the first to admit that he has always been quietly envious of their situation. 'They stay in and eat together of an evening,' he said wistfully of his friends' new lifestyle. 'And that's a nice thing to do when you are in a relationship.'

So why was the tall, good-looking, well-dressed and utterly eligible David still single? In 2005, the year that *Little Britain* really turned into a phenomenon, he admitted that he didn't know. And that it was starting to bother him. 'I would love to have gone through this year with somebody I loved. When lots of extraordinary things are happening to you, it would be lovely to be able to share them,' he told a group of journalists at one celebrity evening, before asking – no one knows how seriously – if anyone had a friend who wanted a date.

In the long term, David's personal ambitions are completely traditional. 'I see marriage as a conversation you're going to have for the rest of your life and I would love to be married – with kids,' he says. 'Ideally, I would have three, because three kids is a gang and I think children get on quite well in a gang.' Finding the right woman to help create this gang wasn't as easy as it might appear, David says. Though anyone with even a passing interest in the gossip columns would know he has hardly been short of practice. The list of Walliams's women is long – and over the years it has driven the tabloids wild. Patsy Kensit, Denise Van Outen, Dannii Minogue,

Martine McCutcheon, Aimee Osbourne, former *Coronation Street* actress Suranne Jones and television presenter Jayne Middlemiss have all been linked to the star – though he has consistently denied dating (or even really meeting) several of them. Those that have been genuinely close to him include signer and model Lisa Moorish, who had previously dated both Liam Gallagher and Pete Doherty. And nurse turned adult television star Abi Titmuss and David really were together for nearly four months – a record for David in recent times. That short but important relationship was different in other ways as well. Instead of parading out on the town as their characters would have suggested, the couple spent a lot of rare nights in, cooking and watching DVDs together, before things seemed to fizzle out and die a natural death. Both say they are still good friends.

David accepts that tabloid rumours are part of the package of being young, famous and single. But he rejects the claims that he is some kind of cruel lothario who takes advantage of his high-profile situation. 'It sometimes looks as if I have been serial dating, but I would gladly have stayed with some of these women,' he says – though he declines to explain exactly which ones he's referring to, or why those relationships foundered.

When they do speak of him, his female friends and former lovers are almost always complimentary – Denise Van Outen, who in early 2006 soaked up the sun with him in the Indian Ocean, says he is 'the kind of man who always calls you a taxi and rings to make sure you get

home safely'. Others are even ready to forge new
professional connections, even after their personal
relationships have ended. One of David's other former
lovers, the model Lisa Snowden, returned to her on/off
partner George Clooney after their relationship had
cooled. But they stayed friends and at a party many
months later she told David that she might have a new
star for his next series. 'George loves the "laydees"
sketches and might even put on a dress if you offered him
a part,' she confided. For the record, David and Matt both
agreed that a star like George Clooney would probably
destroy the balance of an ordinary episode of the show.
That said, they haven't ruled out asking him to appear in
a one-off and particularly star-studded Christmas special
they have been working on for the past couple of years.

As far as some parts of the media were concerned,
David's gentlemanly image wasn't exciting enough,
however. So a new one was created for him. He was
ranked alongside hell-raisers Mickey Rourke and Colin
Farrell, Kevin Pietersen and bad boy Jude Law as one of
the London *Evening Standard*'s 'Top Ten Casanovas of
2005'. The *Daily Mirror*, meanwhile, called him 'the
randiest man on the planet', and like most of the other
tabloids it went wild when David was named in the
divorce papers of an underwear model who split from her
husband in September 2005. Earlier in the year the
model, who had also acted in *Footballers' Wives* and the
Jude Law film *Alfie*, said she had gone back to a hotel
room with David after she had been modelling at the

10th birthday party of lingerie store Agent Provocateur. 'David met her in February and at no stage did she tell him she was married. That is all he has to say,' said his spokesman as the divorce case loomed. The model, however, was more forthcoming: 'I have no money and David won't return my calls,' she claimed. 'Now I feel stupid that I have ruined my marriage for a two-night fling with a TV comedian who wears a dress.'

Worrying that the media frenzy was getting out of control and affecting some of his entirely innocent female friendships, even David ultimately felt the need to call time and calm things down. 'There is an element of the papers simply linking celebrities with anyone else that they can, with pictures and quotes being used to support a fantasy and it's just crazy,' he said. But this didn't stop him being photographed, often in a very touchy-feely manner, with yet more beautiful women at yet more glamorous parties.

The problem for David, if you can call it a problem, was that he had fallen in love with the celebrity world that he had so recently joined. He likes talking shop, he thrives on the company of his fellow professionals and he's desperate to keep a close ear to the ground and know first about any changes in the entertainment universe.

Fortunately for his professional credibility, David didn't turn up when former *Daily Mirror* editor Piers Morgan famously sent a host of stars spoof invitations to the opening night of a new restaurant called The Envelope, just to see who would miss the pun and be desperate enough to turn up. Unfortunately, he had to admit that his seemingly insatiable party spirit meant he might well have been caught out had the invitation made it his way.

And, for all his attempts to act cool, David admits to a childish excitement at the type of places he is now invited to, and the kind of people he meets there. At the 2005 Baftas, for example, he asked guitarist Johnny Marr for his autograph and was thrilled to get the chance to speak to Cate Blanchett and Christian Slater. Other big events give him a similar buzz. 'I went to a party at Sam Taylor-Wood's and the whole thing was literally dripping with famous people,' he says, only partly aware that he had long since become one of them. 'Oh look there's Kate Moss, I thought. There's the Osbournes. There's Lucian Freud. There's Heidi Slimane. There's Elton John. It really was the most extraordinary collection of people. That Kate Moss knows my name is very exciting to me,' he admits, with refreshing honesty. 'When you meet people who you have grown up admiring and watching, you never imagine that you will be sharing social space with them. It might seem very superficial but it feels amazing to be in that world.'

For all his natural ebullience, David does admit that some of his childhood insecurities have never left him. So he struggles sometimes to accept just how easily he fits into the celebrity world. And for all his preening, he also struggles to accept just how good he looks. Fans who get to meet him say David is far better looking in the flesh than he is on screen – and most say he looks pretty good on television anyway. He's the perfect height of six-foot-three, and also wears his clothes well – well enough to be ranked fifth in the *GQ* list of best-dressed men in the summer of 2005. The winner was Rio Ferdinand and, while Jose Mourinho, Jude Law and Clive Owen were ranked above David, he was judged three places higher than former Gucci head of design Tom Ford, an accolade David laughed about for days.

Interestingly enough, the one notable absence from the *GQ* best-dressed list was David Beckham – and David Walliams had a pretty firm opinion about why. 'David Beckham? A style icon? I don't buy it,' he said, letting rip for once. 'He's just a man who buys a lot of new clothes. That isn't style. Style is John Lydon or Quentin Crisp. It's looking like someone extraordinary and standing out on your own. The Libertines' Carl Barât. Andre 3000 in plus fours and a stripy shirt, with an afro. David Bowie in a canary-yellow suit. Gilbert and George. Pet Shop Boys projecting that look of the City gent and his rent boy. Morrissey inventing the cult of the man in vintage dinner jacket and jeans. Franz Ferdinand in Dior Homme. Tom Wolfe in a crisp white poplin suit. That's style. Not opening parcels from Dolce & Gabbana.'

If dressing well and looking good help attract women to David, the thing that really wins him fans is his personality. Far more artistic than the pub-loving, football-focused Matt, David is happy to talk about galleries, films, restaurants, exhibitions and cultural trends. Perhaps more importantly, he doesn't just talk about clothes and shopping – he is ready to put his words into action as well. 'I have always had a strong feminine side, which I have enjoyed and embraced. My favourite thing is to go shopping with girls and watch them try on all sorts of outfits. I love being called on to cast my eyes over other people's clothes. If I hadn't been a comedian I would love to have been a stylist,' he says, an admission few other straight men would be prepared to make. Which brings us round to the endlessly debated question of David's true sexuality.

Most commentators agree that, if a group of people who knew nothing about them were shown a talk-show interview with Matt and David and asked which of the two was gay, they would automatically pick David. And that's aside from the infamous *Parkinson* show on which David and Will Young danced a foxtrot and faked a snog before Will sat on David's knee. As far as Matt and David are concerned, one loves football, the other loves fashion. One stays home almost every night; the other prefers to hit the parties. One says he wears women's dresses for a living; the other says he wears them because he likes it. If you are thinking in terms of stereotypes, then it's not hard to see why David gets the gay vote every time. Throw in the fact that he loves camping it up when he talks – and that he likes talking, full stop – and the jury is likely to rest.

David's flamboyance has long since been raising eyebrows among journalists. The *Sun* famously created a Gay-o-meter that swung from blue to pink on a daily basis according to David's latest exploits – appearing at a Kylie concert (twice) put him in the pink zone, while being snapped outside a restaurant with what the paper liked to call 'a mystery woman' moved him back to blue, for example. The Will Young snog on *Parkinson* blew the machine up, the *Sun* claimed.

For a while, David was happy to play along with the joke – and like many straight men with gay friends he felt he would be insulting them if he started to make official denials about his own status. David was also prepared to admit that he did play to the gallery sometimes. 'Most women think I'm gay, so I have a really easy time with them,' he joked when the questions about his sexuality first arose.

But as time passed the joke did start to wear a little thin. The worst moment, David says, was when Jonathan Ross was hosting the British Comedy Awards in 2004. The event was being broadcast live on television when Ross said, of Matt, that 'There's some speculation that he isn't the only gay in the double act.' Sitting in the audience with his father and other family members David, for once, had a minor sense-of-humour failure.

Over the coming months, he would certainly live to regret his endlessly mis-quoted statement that he was 'only 70 per cent heterosexual'. That means he's actually gay, the rumours said. But it didn't. The comment actually referred to a joke magazine quiz in which you ticked boxes and listed your hobbies and cultural and sporting interests to define how 'masculine' you were. Nothing in the survey covered sexual attraction at all. 'Matt turns out to be straighter than I do and apparently I need to stop going to the opera and wearing frocks and dancing to Britney,' David joked with a reporter when the quiz came up in conversation. Several years later, with the original context of the story forgotten, he came to regret his candour and began to despair of being endlessly described as '30 per cent gay'. With hindsight, he also says describing his home as looking 'like Liberace's holiday home' could have sent out the wrong signals as well.

So his hunt for a girlfriend continued. And for all the contradictions in David's personal life, his friends were convinced that he would soon find one – not least because they say he is an old-fashioned and decent bloke at heart. According to the experts, he had more going for him than his good looks and female-friendly hobbies too. Apparently, being a comedian was the perfect weapon in the contest to find a mate. 'Magazine surveys are forever telling us that, out of all the qualities that a woman might seek in a man, making her laugh is at the top of the list. It triumphs over good looks, wealth and economic stability,' says psychoanalyst and author Darian Leader. 'Changes in society mean that the old macho values have worn thin. The self-deprecating clownish joker might seem the most honest alternative to the lost male hero. Rather than pretending to have macho qualities, he shows his weaknesses, even draws attention to them.' It is an analysis that could have been written specifically to describe the David Walliams approach to life.

So what kind of woman might win David's heart? It's a tough question to answer, not least because he himself admits that older women appeal to him as much as younger starlets. He says he has always had a huge crush on Lauren Bacall, the 80-year-old star of Hollywood's golden era. Even Matt's mother Diana has been the target of some of his (hopefully humorous) public comments, in an echo of the 'Jason and Nan' sketches from *Little Britain*. 'Matt and I often talk about what it would be like if I actually started going out with her,' David said once. Diana Lucas, for her part, has always refused to comment.

And for all his jokes and bravado over women, David can still come a cropper. A throwaway comment about fancying everyone in Girls Aloud fell flat when they turned up their collective noses at someone they suggested was already over the hill. Fortunately, if David needed any reassurance that he had the means and the manner to overcome this kind of setback then he need only take a look at his house keys. The money from *Little Britain* allowed him to spend an estimated £3.25 million buying a fantastic new home in London – and not just any house. The boy from a Reigate semi bought the old Supernova Heights, ex-home of Oasis frontman Noel Gallagher and his wife Meg Mathews. Fixtures and fittings there included the infamous £30,000 mosaic bath, the three-tonne floor to ceiling aquarium in the hall and the priceless reputation as party central in the Britpop years.

After the Gallaghers moved out, the house had been

owned by ex-*Hollyoaks* actress Davinia Taylor – and David was to face some gentle ribbing over his lack of rock star – or soap star – attitude when he moved in and immediately applied to the council for permission to build a desperately middle-class conservatory in the back garden. In another odd coincidence, David found he wasn't alone in playing celebrity house-swap by buying Noel Gallagher's old home. At almost exactly the same time, Vic Reeves bought Tom Baker's old house in Kent, having previously lived in a property once owned by Noël Coward's agent. It seemed that at David's level a house wasn't worth looking at unless it had celebrity connections – and ideally a *Little Britain* link.

David went on to push the celebrity point even further by buying a classic 1966 Mercedes from artist Sam Taylor-Wood (one of his close friends, her increasingly valuable framed photographs have pride of place in his bedroom). If chocolate is Matt's secret vice, cars are David's. In *Little Britain* it had been his idea to put a copy of *Top Gear* in Emily's bedroom when she was trying to persuade a lodger of her credentials as a laydee. And in 2005 he got the chance to go on the show itself. After some dodgy turns in the practice circuit he raced around the show's track in 1 minute 50.7 seconds, putting him just ahead of the likes of Sir Ranulph Fiennes, Eddie Izzard and Steve Coogan in the celebrity time trial. And he got more than just a great day out talking cars with the likes of Jeremy Clarkson and Richard Hammond – the producers also agreed to waive the show's usual fee and lend him his dream car (a 'James Bond-style' Aston Martin DB6) for a weekend instead.

The man who had famously said he struggles to bond with other men was gradually finding some good new mates as well. Robbie Williams, who presented the Best Comedians prize to David and Matt at the GQ Awards at the Royal Opera House in September 2005, was one of them. David had first met the singer when he had recorded some voice-overs for Robbie's *Live in Your Living Room* tour in 1998. Since then they had laughed about the *Rock Profile* sketches and stayed in touch ever since.

So David was one of the specially invited guests at the showcase gig Robbie gave at the Astoria in London to road test some of the songs from his forthcoming *Intensive Care* album (rarely for him, Matt had also turned up to the event, accompanied by partner Kevin). Away from the spotlight, David and Robbie had been joking about working together ever since the Comic Relief sketch the previous year and there were rumours that they might be writing up some comedy lyrics for a new-direction album to be released in 2007.

David's love of the celebrity circuit was paying dividends on the work front as well. He told so many of his famous friends of his ambition of having a bit part in *EastEnders* that it was only a matter of time before word got back to the show's producers, for example. So, after the briefest and most informal audition, he got offered the kind of part most actors would kill for. Firstly, he was playing the best friend of one of the show's leading characters, Alfie Moon, so he had a high profile from the start. Secondly, his scenes were being shown over the ratings-topping Christmas season of 2003, as the climax of one of the soap's longest-running plot lines – the love lives of Alfie and Kat Slater. Thirdly, and most importantly, David achieved two of what the soap's cast call 'doff doffers' – when you are the last person to speak before the show's theme tune cuts in at the end of a show. It was, he says, a dream come true. And he says he has tried to leave the door open for a repeat visit at some point in the future.

With that done, he was also determined to do more straight drama whenever he was on a break from *Little Britain* – ideally alongside the best actors he could find. So he signed to appear alongside the likes of Zoë Wanamaker, Derek Jacobi, Simon Callow, Amanda Holden and Ian Richardson in *Marple: The Body In The Library*, the first of the new-look Agatha Christie adaptations that were filmed in 2004. It was a serious role, but David did take a typically light-hearted approach to it – not least by modelling his character on maverick Tory MP Boris Johnson. 'When I first read the script Boris Johnson kept popping into my head. Here is someone, I think, who could either be perceived as very, very clever, or very, very, stupid.' Perhaps fortunately for Boris, David refused to say if he ever came to any conclusion on the issue.

For all the extra-curricular activities that both Matt and David were doing beyond the confines of *Little Britain*, they did stick together when it came to talking about the work. Their agents were getting an increasing number of requests for individual interviews, photo-shoots and appearances as their solo achievements began to mount up. But almost all of them were turned down – because at that time the men didn't enjoy facing the media on their own.

Psychologists who watched the first high-profile interviews the pair gave in the late 1990s say it was obvious that neither of them was comfortable with the chat-show process. 'Both men would constantly try to find ways to bring funny voices, impressions or other distractions into the conversation. They wanted to be in character as often as possible so they didn't have to be themselves,' says psychologist and author Kim Davis. 'At the end of almost every sentence they also glance very quickly at each other for reassurance – and they both look grateful when the other one actually steps in and finishes their sentences for them, which they do all the time. Overall, it was as if, despite the success that they had achieved, they still didn't quite feel that they had a right to be on a chat show or that anyone would be interested in them as individuals.' David, leaving the set of BBC3's little-watched *The Ralph Little Show*, confirmed that assessment. 'Pull on a wig and some glasses and it's easy being on stage. This is terrifying,' he confided to the production staff.

As time passed, some subtle changes became apparent in the way the men behaved on the chat-show circuit, however. Matt continued to do most of the talking when it came to their work, happy to explain how they filmed certain shots, how they wrote their scripts or created their characters. But somehow his body language was still uncomfortable. He tended to sit on the edge of his seat, his eyes suggesting that for all the jokes and the anecdotes he was counting the seconds until he could get out of the spotlight and back into the real world. Viewers also noticed he was one of the few chat-show guests in modern Britain polite enough to use the words 'sorry to interrupt, but...' when he has a point he wants to get across.

David, meanwhile, seemed to have developed a taste for talking about broader issues. So he was the one who would talk about other programmes and performers – and about his personal life. And his body language was becoming increasingly confident. He was able to sit back, stretch out and relax on the guest sofas, his earlier need for wigs and glasses long since forgotten.

The combination of these two approaches meant that the pair were a popular choice with the bookers who tried to arrange high-profile guests for the likes of Michael Parkinson, Jonathan Ross and their peers. True, Matt and David turned down the vast majority of invitations, but the bookers didn't give up. 'If we couldn't get the men themselves we decided to aim for the next best thing – their mothers,' as ITV booker Charlotte Marling put it. Matt and David's families had grown close over the years, with Matt's mother Diana and David's mother Kathleen becoming particularly close friends. So, when Matt and David couldn't make it to the 2005 National Television Awards, it seemed a natural choice for their mothers to take their places. The two women took to the star-studded event as if to the manor born, happily going up on stage and making short speeches when their sons were named as award-winners.

The mothers were also there to watch when their sons were immortalised at Madame Tussaud's in London. In the spring of 2005, the museum had revealed the names of the stars its visitors most wanted added to the roster – Matt and David were ahead by a mile. So, at £100,000 a piece and requiring three months of work, the models were commissioned. Matt and David decided to be moulded as Lou and Andy and turned up in character for the unveiling ceremony. 'I don't like it. Prefer that one,' was, of course, Matt's response as Andy, when David's Lou tried to coax even the briefest 'thank you' from him.

As the photographs of the Madame Tussaud's unveiling hit the next day's newspapers, several journalists commented that the real-life Matt and David looked a lot worse than their waxworks. And the men could hardly deny that they were exhausted. They were in the middle of the intensive rehearsals for the live show and reckoned they had just squeezed 12 months of work into eight by writing and filming the third series of *Little Britain* in record time. In the editing suite, they were both convinced that the new series was a winner. While writing it, they had particularly enjoyed putting a few of their favourite characters in some radically different situations, and they were convinced that some of the new characters were strong enough to be classics. The production team had loved it and the fan base was desperate to see the new shows. But, as they signed off each episode, Matt and David found it impossible to relax.

The new series was due to start on 17 November on BBC1 after yet another massive promotional campaign. It felt like make-or-break time all over again.

CHAPTER 15

MRS EMERY AND BEYOND

I s an incontinent old woman really something to laugh about? The bad-taste arguments were back with a vengeance as soon as *Little Britain*'s third series hit the screens. One of the biggest issues was over the incontinent Mrs Emery, who graphically lost control in shops, libraries, doctors' surgeries and anywhere else Matt and David could think of to film her.

A large – probably young – slice of the show's audience thought the sketches were fantastic. But many more were horrified, so Matt and David soon found themselves back on the defensive. The first accusation to fight off was that this was lazy one-trick-pony comedy. Critics said that once you had seen one Mrs Emery scene you had seen them all, because each of them ended exactly the same way. 'But the inevitability is partly the point,' David said in defence (secretly loving the fact that he was making people squirm on their sofas as they waited to see exactly when the waters would break). 'People like repetition.

They like visual jokes. Simple things make people laugh. Perhaps children or old people falling over shouldn't be funny but a lot of the time it is. We just take that one stage further.'

On a more subtle level, the men also argued that there was something else going on in the Mrs Emery sketches. The real point of them, as in so much of Matt and David's comedy, was not the actual incontinence but the way other people reacted to it. Just as cutaway reaction shots to Jamie Theakston in *Rock Profile* had emphasised the weirdness of their pop-star caricatures, so the real focus of the Mrs Emery scenes was on the way the various neighbours, librarians and GPs pretended that nothing was happening.

As far as Matt and David are concerned, the sketches are uncomfortable viewing because deep down we all wonder if we too would be typically British and pretend nothing was wrong when the waterworks started. If we were faced with someone like this in real life, would we also try to just finish our conversations and walk away, without making a scene? Matt and David reckon we would – so when they are being serious they say they wanted to film the incontinence scenes to try and make us address those thoughts. When they are being honest, they also admit they did it to raise some guilty laughs and grab a few headlines.

'We wanted people to go into work the next day and say that they couldn't believe what we had done,' says David. 'And it's actually quite hard to shock people now.

We've seen people have sex on telly and everything, so getting complaints is a lot harder than you would think. We're on the edge at times but I think people realise we are trying to be funny and not offensive because if it's just shocking then we're not doing our job properly.' He also says that when the media storm is over he believes that even *Little Britain*'s most extreme characters may end up in the comedy mainstream – as has happened to so many of the *bêtes noirs* of the past. 'Whatever the columnists say, British people love their comedy to be on the edge. Like Basil Fawlty doing the goose step, Mr Creosote in *The Meaning of Life* when he explodes, and *The Young Ones*. We love really rude humour in this country even if we think we shouldn't.'

For his part, Matt says the criticism over characters like Mrs Emery is misdirected because it's always coming at them second-hand. 'It's people thinking they should be shocked on someone else's behalf. The truth is that kids love rudeness. Old people love rudeness, people of our age love rudeness. So where are all the people who don't like it? I'm not sure they exist any more. We always find people respond positively to the racier parts. They find it liberating.' He also points to a long British history of pushing the boundaries of taste to raise a laugh. 'It is a sort of very British vulgarity that goes back to McGill's postcards and smutty *Carry On* humour. People have always liked that, probably always will.'

Whether this sort of thing was suitable for children was another matter, however. Teachers across the country said

Little Britain's catchphrases were being repeated by even the youngest children – and some heads even wrote to parents asking them to respect the 9pm watershed and ban their kids from seeing the show. A *Radio Times* survey showed this wasn't working. More than 86,000 four- to nine-year-olds were watching alongside 280,000 ten- to fifteen-year-olds – even though the British Board of Film Classification had given the first two series a 15 rating. Matt and David weren't sure what they could do about it – and David in particular was secretly pleased that they were so popular with kids. 'The show isn't designed or meant for children but it is great that they love it,' he said. 'When I was at school I was watching *The Young Ones*. I was probably about 12 and *The Young Ones* certainly wasn't meant for 12-year-olds, but there is always that element in kids where they want to watch the naughty comedy that's not meant for them.'

In fact, Matt and David had recently received a confidence-booster to help them ride out all the latest media storms: they had just faced down their first piece of official criticism – and won. The challenge had come with the announcement of a series of investigations by broadcasting regulator Ofcom. 'We have had 24 complaints relating to the show. Five for mocking the disabled, four for bad language, two for general taste and decency, three for harmful portrayal of the elderly, one for religious offence and nine for racial offence,' said Ofcom's Simon Bates. Fortunately for Matt and David, none of them was upheld.

The regulator wasn't the only one to give the pair a clean bill of health – two special-interest groups came forward to say that they too stood by the comedians. Firstly, David Allison of gay rights group Outrage confirmed that they had no issues with Daffyd. 'A portrayal of a limp-wristed poof with a handbag would be offensive. But Matt Lucas's character is so far removed from anyone I know that it is funny. It is so camp that it is actually a positive image,' he said. Others agreed with him – Daffyd became the unofficial mascot of the 2005 Sydney Mardi Gras festival.

Weight Watchers' spokeswoman Fern Milne was equally relaxed about the Marjorie Dawes character. 'Marjorie is just a comedy character on a very popular programme. She is an extreme caricature and our meetings are obviously very different to hers,' she said, shrugging off claims that the show might lead to a reduction in attendance at real-life classes.

It seemed that ordinary people were prepared to give Matt and David the benefit of the doubt and accept them for what they are – comedians. As the third series of the show would prove, they are also two of the hardest-working comedians in the business. There were more than two dozen different characters on display in the first few episodes of the new series alone. So, whatever else they were criticised for, you couldn't say Matt and David didn't give value for money.

Those characters included the usual mix of new and old. Newcomers Ting Tong and Mr Dudley were popular from the start and viewers liked the fact that their storyline moved so quickly – within weeks of her arrival Ting Tong had moved her mother into Mr Dudley's council flat and would ultimately turf him out by transforming it into a fully functioning Thai restaurant while he was out at the shops.

Some decent visual gags also helped with the pacing of the new shows. One of the best examples was when Emily and Florence go into a pub to loudly announce to their fellow drinkers that Florence was on her last night of freedom 'as a single lay-dee' before getting married. Anyone who wants one last chance to chat her up – or more – should speak now or forever hold their peace, trilled Emily in excited expectation. The camera cuts to a lone male drinker at a corner table who, in the ensuing silence, holds up and drops a pin.

The guest list on the new shows was as starry as ever – headed by Oscar-nominated actress Imelda Staunton, who said she had wanted a role on the show from the first time she had seen it. The men were finally able to oblige when they decided Andy might need a new carer for a few days while Lou was on a break. Imelda was the no-nonsense Irish home help who refused to let Andy watch television, forced him to help with the cleaning and – in the final scene – got pushed off the edge of a cliff.

Rob Brydon was also there in another set of cameos alongside Bubbles de Vere and her love rival Desiree. Watching him squeezed into a sauna alongside the naked ladies was somehow almost as uncomfortable as seeing

Mrs Emery do her stuff in an earlier scene, according to commentaries on one *Little Britain* fansite.

Some of the other new characters and scenes made less of an impression, however. Sir Norman Fry was widely seen as one of the least successful. Played by David, with Matt as his 'tweeds and twin set' wife, Sir Norman was the kind of politician who drags his family to meet the press at the bottom of his drive every time he has to explain away an episode of sexual misconduct. His extraordinarily convoluted and unconvincing excuses did sometimes raise a laugh, but critics had a point when they said the character was a throwback to the last Conservative government – so it felt nearly a decade out of date.

And were some of the more established characters also past their sell-by date in 2005? Former fans said Sebastian, who had started life as a tragic figure, full of pathos and unrequited love for his boss, had become an unsubtle, manipulative monster by the time series three drew to a close. All the usual slapstick and bawdy humour was still there in his scenes. But was there the same depth? Having acted so outrageously and made his desires so obvious, where could the character go from there?

Of course, as the third series was broadcast there was a theory that Sebastian didn't have anywhere else to go – and neither did any of the other *Little Britain* characters. For some time there had been rumours that this was to be the final series of the show. Fans were convinced that Matt and David would quit while they were ahead and move on to pastures new. Knowing when to stop was a tactic that had worked well for John Cleese with *Fawlty Towers* and Ricky Gervais with *The Office*, and the general view was that Matt and David wouldn't want to outstay their welcome either. But, while conspiracy theorists reckoned they saw plenty of clues in the final Christmas Eve episode, Matt and David were determined to keep all their options open.

So, while fans said they spotted a Hitchcock-style goodbye when David played himself in the last Vicky Pollard sketch of the series, he said he was simply having fun – and was glad not to have to spend hours in make-up and costumes before a scene. In the same episode, fans also reckoned they saw the end of an era when Florence turned up on Emily's doorstep to say his wife wouldn't let him see her any more. 'Together we fooled the world,' Emily cried, wrong as ever, in what sounded like another big goodbye. But, as it turned out, Florence weakened and slipped back into Emily's house to try on just one more dress while her wife sat in the car. A fat laydee had not yet sung, so perhaps the double act wasn't over.

The biggest tease of all came with a cleverly leaked story that in the final episode of the series Daffyd was going to leave the village and head to London. Had that happened then his character would, almost certainly, be history. Being one of maybe a million gays in a city was unlikely to be as funny as being the only one in the village. But while Daffyd did indeed pack his suitcase and headed to the station with Myfanwy, he then lost his nerve and headed back for home. It seemed that Llanddewi Breffi would live to see another day.

When they were put on the spot and asked if *Little Britain* was all over, Matt and David were both determined to stay upbeat. 'As long as David and I enjoy working together we will carry on. Ultimately, we want to carry on making shows for as long as people want to watch them and, if the latest shows are anything to go by, they do,' said Matt of a possible fourth series.

'I wouldn't want to do this if it wasn't fun any more,' confirmed David at the same time. 'But it is fun and I think we will carry on for as long as people want to see us doing it.'

Viewing figures suggested that the demand was certainly there. The first episode of the new series had attracted its highest ever audience of 10.17 million viewers back in November, with more than four in ten of all viewers tuning in. Figures fell over the weeks, as normally happens with a new series, but they picked up again for the final Christmas Eve show, which attracted more than two million people – more than the likes of *Ant and Dec's Christmas Takeaway* and the *Stars in Their Eyes Celebrity Special*.

And the pair reckoned they had one key trick up their sleeves that would keep *Little Britain* fresh for a lot longer than the doubters predicted. Both were well aware that individual characters from ensemble casts could often translate successfully to a larger stage in shows of their own. They had also liked the way the later *League of*

Gentlemen shows had moved on from quick-fire sketches to longer and more detailed scenes. Bringing several of the disparate characters together, as that show had done, seemed to work. So while there were obvious difficulties in putting Vicky Pollard in the same sketch as Daffyd Thomas, or putting Sebastian alongside Emily Howard, Matt and David stored away the idea for future use.

They also wanted to make it clear that no one should draw any conclusions from the fact that a full fourth series wasn't being talked about from the moment the third one ended. 'It takes nearly a year to film a new series and with the live tour taking up so much of 2006 we always knew it would be impossible to film one that year as well,' said David. 'We probably won't be making plans for 2007 until the tour is over at the earliest.'

And it wasn't as if the pair weren't as busy as ever – or that they weren't still storing up ideas for new characters and scenarios. For all the madness surrounding them as their fame hit new heights, both men knew they had to stay grounded if they wanted to stay funny.

'The important thing is not to get too giddy or carried away with it all,' says Matt. 'A comic has to keep on living a real life, otherwise he will have nothing to draw on. You can't start doing routines about being upgraded or getting a good table in a restaurant because people can't buy into it. You see it happening to bands. Singing about record-company bosses and drugs and losing touch with their audience.' Matt remains determined to keep things as real as possible. 'I still get the bus everywhere, there's no reason not to,' he claimed as the live show reached its halfway point.

David agreed with his friend's sentiments, though he was nowhere near as keen on the idea of travelling by bus. 'If you stop meeting people on a level with them then you're not going to be able to observe so much, which means you are not going to be able to create so well,' he reflected. So he continued to try and live an ordinary life, drinking coffee outside his local café in north London, shopping on Oxford Street and seeing plays in Shaftesbury Avenue with friends.

In the process, he says, the great British public certainly didn't let him get above himself. 'Hey, you look like the guy who does the thing with the bald guy,' was a frequent comment David heard as he went about his daily routine. Matt, meanwhile, says he can hardly count the times people come up to him and say, 'I love your character. "Am I bothered? Look at my face, I'm not bothered." You're brilliant, you are.' Which would be nice, of course, except for the fact that this is rival comic Catherine Tate's catchphrase.

The one other thing the men were determined not to do once they hit the big time was to hit the bottle – or worse. Both had read biographies of all the famous comics who had turned to alcohol and drugs to beat off the depression that haunts the entertainment industry. Having got on well with Michael Barrymore years earlier, they had watched in horror as drink and other demons conspired to end his career. Thankfully, anecdotal evidence suggests that neither Matt nor David is likely to follow this pattern. When they both went down to Rye in East Sussex for a friend's stag weekend, for example, their overriding memory of the occasion was not of getting drunk or drugged up and chaining the naked groom-to-be to a lamppost, but of going on a ghost walk led by what seemed to be the oldest lady in the town – a character who had already been stored away for use in a future sketch.

They are also determined not to rise to the bait of newspaper reporters and comment on any rival performers or shows. The reasons for their reticence are simple. It took them ten long, hard and doubt-filled years to make their mark in the entertainment business. They faced a lot of critics on their way to the top of the industry tree. They know what it is like to be battered by the critics and by fellow professionals. And they don't want to make others suffer the same heartaches or insecurities. 'It's really hard to make people laugh consistently and I respect everyone who succeeds in doing it,' said Matt, fending off yet another question about their comedy colleagues. 'There are things I don't like, certainly, but I'd choose not to say what they are because it would be of no benefit – not to me, nor to the person I was criticising. It would seem mean-spirited and, anyway, everything comes down to personal taste.'

Of all the official interviews they have given over the years, and all the off-the-cuff comments made to reporters in the street and at public events, very few could hurt any rival performer's feelings. And even Peter Andre and Jordan would probably have laughed along when Matt once said sarcastically that an invitation to their 2005 wedding (which neither Matt nor David received) 'would make our fame worthwhile'.

Ultimately, both men are still as far from being prima donnas of the entertainment world as it is possible to get. Both are fully aware of the reality of the fame game and the obligations it puts them under. 'You spend your whole life trying to get attention, to get on TV, and then you moan as soon as you are because someone shouted, "I'm a lady!" at you in the street. That would be pretty churlish, wouldn't it? It seems like a very small price to pay for the opportunity to make your show,' says David. 'Basically, we have been able to take licence-fee money to indulge my desire to dress up as women and to show off.'

Along the way, both men felt they had managed to slay some of their childhood demons – though with slightly different results. For David, the dressing up and the showing off had become an end in itself – he enjoyed it and wanted to carry on doing it because it was fun. For Matt, the process remained both a mask and a job. 'Personally, I wouldn't mind if I were never photographed as myself ever again. Comedy isn't an escape for me, it's simply the only thing I can do. I'm not very bright, I'm always late, I'm really clumsy, just a twit, really. The kick I get is coming out of make-up and costume, looking in the mirror and seeing someone different. When I did the Rev Jessie King with a fake nose, lips and teeth, I couldn't see myself. It's being able to hide, or to be grotesque and get away with it. What I enjoy is the idea of being someone else. The presence of an audience or a camera legitimises your behaviour. If you're mild mannered you can become incredibly rude or daft or incredibly emotional because you are being someone else.'

So, with a fourth series of *Little Britain* at least a year away, who would the men want to be next? Despite the grind of the hundred-plus dates on their live tour, both were making new plans on a near-daily basis. And both knew that they might as well take advantage of their fame and bring as many of those plans into action while they had the clout to do so. 'Most comedians have their moment and ours is happening right now. The trick is to enjoy it before fashion moves on,' Matt said as the pair were featured on the Christmas Day edition of the highbrow *South Bank Show* and a year-end survey once again named them as the most powerful people in the entertainment industry.

That power meant Matt, a lifelong fan of the late composer Lionel Bart, was able to record a tribute to him for Radio Two. It was exactly the kind of relatively low-profile project he could never have got off the ground when he had been a struggling and unknown stand-up comedian. What made the experience even sweeter was that when he did make the show he was able to collaborate on it with Barbara Windsor, one of his other comedy heroines from the *Carry On* era. 'She was so, so sweet about *Little Britain* and I felt as honoured to meet her as I would the Queen,' says an unusually expansive Matt. Another bonus from that job was that he could subsequently introduce Barbara to his star-struck mother. 'It's a great little by-product of success that you get to meet people you have watched and admired for years and that they know who you are and want to talk to you,' Matt said of his newfound celebrity status. But he refused to get carried away by it. 'You have to remember that you are only there because of the work and that you have to keep on doing it,' he added more soberly.

Researching Lionel Bart's life for the tribute had also reawakened another of Matt's long-held ambitions – to write a West End musical. Andrew Lloyd Webber, no less, had just said he would be ready to back a project based on the *Little Britain* characters. But Matt was already looking in other directions. He was planning some co-production deals aimed at translating existing stage shows and films into musicals and he was constantly making notes about an entirely new production of his own. Getting an original musical on stage is a huge task nowadays, requiring a multi-million war chest of cash from backers. But all Matt's other career dreams had come true and he was convinced that in time he could bring this one to fruition too.

Unfortunately, Lloyd Webber and Ben Elton had already attempted to fuse Matt's two great loves – musicals and football – in the short-lived West End show *The Beautiful Game*. Could the two subjects be joined together in a different – and more successful – way? he wondered. As an occasional freelance writer for *Total Football* magazine (another dream job that Matt was convinced he would never have acquired if he hadn't been famous), he did at least feel he had his finger on the football pulse. Adding music would be a long-term challenge. And while it may come to nothing, it would be a happy dream while it lasted.

For his part, David was also being linked to some projects close to his heart. When Christopher Eccleston had given up the new *Doctor Who* role after just one series, David was widely touted as a possible replacement. In reality, he had been too busy with *Little Britain* to even consider it, and the man who did get the job, David Tennant, now looks set to keep it for many years. But if Tennant moved on in a few years' time? David left the idea of a takeover bid hanging in the air – though in some respects, it seemed as if the idea of winning the role wouldn't actually be enough for him: 'Ever since I was a child I have wanted to be Doctor Who,' he says. 'Not to play Doctor Who. To *be* Doctor Who.'

Moving up a gear, there were even rumours that David might one day make a good James Bond – especially as newcomer Daniel Craig's grasp on the role seemed uncertain. When *Little Britain* had first been filmed, David had got a close-up look at what the big-screen job might entail. He had visited the set where Pierce Brosnan and Madonna had been filming the fencing scenes for *Die Another Day*. 'Brilliant to watch,' David enthused, on the workings of such a big-budget film set – though he also said he might be better cast, and have more fun, as a megalomaniac villain rather than as the hero of the hour.'

Whether or not he ever got a call from the Bond producers, David was certainly aiming to do more films, as soon as his schedule allowed. In 2006, he had two scenes alongside his old friends Steve Coogan and Rob Brydon in the critically acclaimed *A Cock and Bull Story* and he told his agents to keep their eyes open for similar opportunities in the future. Something else he said at the same time suggested that they may ultimately be able to cast a very wide net when finding him suitable roles – he claimed his long-term goal was to become a woman. 'When I'm 60, I like the idea of having a sex change. I would really enjoy having the last ten years of my life as a batty old woman who fills her days with day trips to Deal and spends the evenings at bingo.' As usual, David said it with a smile. But, as there is usually a germ of truth in all of his humour, a fair few of his friends were prepared to bet that it might one day come true.

One thing was for certain: there would be more joint projects with Matt – with a West End stage debut top of the list for the future. 'The play we would love to be in together is *The Dresser*,' says David. 'I would love the title role of the dresser with Matt as the impossible actor-manager he works for. It is a play we have both loved since our days at the National Youth Theatre together.' And there is precedent for comedy favourites taking on the challenge. Nicholas Lyndhurst tried to shake off his

Only Fools and Horses image by starring in the play in London's West End in 2005. And *The Dresser*'s writer, Ronald Harwood, said he was 'a great fan' of *Little Britain* and was certain the pair would do a fantastic job in the roles performed on the big screen by Albert Finney and Tom Courtenay. On a lighter note, the other double act Matt and David wanted to tackle was an appearance on a 'duos edition' of *Celebrity Stars in Their Eyes* (they wanted to reprise their roles as Simon and Garfunkel from *Rock Profile*, though they admitted that many of their younger fans might not recognise the musical duo).

Of course, the one thing the men would never have to do again was worry about money. *Little Britain*, the show that had paid them just £100 a week when it was launched on Radio Four, had since turned into an extraordinary cash cow. The live tour alone was said to have earned the pair a staggering £5 million each – not least because, as well as providing the perfect place to sell all the existing DVDs and other goods, it too was to be sold as a DVD when it ended.

And demand for every previous *Little Britain* DVD had been voracious. The DVD of the first series topped the sales charts and ended up selling more than 1.3 million copies. The second series was released at the height of *Little Britain* mania in October 2005 and both Amazon and HMV said it was easily outselling the first. With the scripts getting into the hardback top tens and the radio series still selling around 30,000 copies a year some five years after they were first broadcast, it is easy to see why the tills are ringing so loudly. And experts say the shows themselves are only the tip of a very lucrative iceberg. The pair approved more than two dozen different *Little Britain*-related T-shirts and sweatshirts, with slogans ranging from 'Nan lover' and 'What a kerfuffle!' to 'Want that one' and 'I am the only gay in the village' – which was, of course available in pink. A £5 mousemat emblazoned with 'Computer says no…' was an obvious idea, and you could also buy mugs, metal and rubber key rings, beanie hats, calendars and pyjamas – the list went on and to try and satisfy demand (and ring up some extra sales) the pair agreed that, as well as having an official website for the show and their tour, they should have a separate one for their online shop as well.

The professionals said that, when it came to making money, the pair were on top of their game. 'Matt and David have a sound marketing strategy to exploit their 15 minutes of fame,' said PR expert Mark Borkowski. 'The fact that they have retained the merchandising rights shows they know what they are doing. The possibilities are endless – from Lou and Andy wheelchairs to Marjorie Dawes diet books. But the men have earned the right to do this because they have played the roles through the years.'

For their part, Matt and David tried to keep all these marketing initiatives in perspective. They also said that one of the reasons for launching the official online store, and for offering so much merchandise at each theatre on their tour, was to stop fans being ripped off by buying the vast number of low-quality fake goods available elsewhere. Making money, the men said, was never their main intention. 'I have never read a contract in my life,' David claimed when asked about all the spin-off ventures. 'I think it is good not to get too involved in the business side of things.' For his part, Matt says the pair were offered a 'life-changing' amount of money to do a commercial in 2005 but turned it down because they thought it would seem tacky.

That said, the sheer volume of official as well as fake merchandising did trigger some bad feeling in the entertainment industry. And both men were hurt that some of the strongest criticism seemed to come from Ricky Gervais, one of the contemporaries they admire more than anyone else. Ricky didn't mention Matt or David by name when he lashed out against profiteering comedians. But, as he was speaking just after the *Little Britain* tour opened and its unprecedented merchandising bonanza got under way, it was easy to guess who was on his mind.

'I get angry when I see people selling their soul, selling their arse,' he told *Guardian* reporter Owen Gibson – and adding that comedians who do this may well lose out in the long run. 'If you look at comedy as a career, it is foolish to go all out. Instead, you've got to hold out. We resisted putting out loads of rubbish from *The Office* for years and years. There was a dancing toy they wanted us to put out. It might be funny to have a tacky Brent doll and it would probably sell well. But it's a con. It's a piece of tat that you don't need.'

Thinking too much about making money and pleasing the marketing boys wouldn't help anyone stay in the comedy business, he continued. 'We are very conscious about the legacy. We're very conscious of it being timeless and universal.' Others, he said, were taking a far easier option. Saying that the best American comedy knocked spots off home-grown shows he said, 'There's something very parochial about a lot of British comedians. Their ambition is to get on a chat show or have *This is Your Life* or a *South Bank Show* made about them. All the things I don't want to do because it's about me as opposed to the work. In Britain, it is always catchphrase comedy or a central character who is a buffoon and always ends up back at square one. I see programmes in England and think, You're aiming low there, you're selling out there, or You got a laugh last time so you've done it again. Sometimes I think, Shame on you, from a production point of view.'

What made Matt and David feel even more sensitive when they read these comments was that they had indeed just filmed a *South Bank Show* — which was to be screened on ITV on Christmas Day. As seemed to happen with almost everything Matt and David got involved with at around this time, the project was controversial from the start. Host Melvyn Bragg was roundly criticised for even thinking of putting the *Little Britain* stars in his arts show. But, to his credit, he refused to accept that comedians didn't sit well alongside his other recent subjects, such as violin virtuoso Maxim Vengerov and theatre director Sir

Peter Hall. 'It is preposterous that anyone would even think that we are dumbing down because we are featuring Matt Lucas and David Walliams. From the very beginning *The South Bank Show* has done features on high-quality artists from across the spectrum. People like John Cleese and Billy Connolly have featured and I think that *Little Britain* is squarely in that area,' he declared.

Bragg went on to rank Matt and David alongside the stars of *The Goon Show* as people capable of 'hitting new heights of comedy'. When filming the show itself, he had no trouble attracting a broad range of contributors, from Ronnie Corbett and Barry Humphries to Imelda Staunton. In the interest of balance, however, he also took a sounding from some of the pair's biggest critics, including film director Ken Russell, who had still not forgiven them for spitting on Vanessa Feltz. Interestingly enough, the one person who didn't appear on the *South Bank Show* to complain about the men was Vanessa herself. Like almost everyone else Matt and David had ever worked with, she had nothing but praise for them. And as the years went by both men were becoming increasingly proud of how their shows were able to help other people build fantastic careers in the entertainment industry.

It is a sign of how genuinely well liked the pair are that the credits on their early shows could almost be repeated verbatim for those from several years later. People who start off working with Matt and David tend to stick with them – and it's said that a real family atmosphere has developed on the other side of the cameras. The hair, make-up and costume workers have enjoyed particularly good recognition in the industry for their efforts. Lisa Cavalli-Green, for example, who first worked with Matt on *Shooting Stars* and with the pair of them on *Rock Profile*, won a Bafta and two Royal Television Society Awards for her work creating all the right looks on *Little Britain*.

They have also proved to be very fair to other professionals whose paths they have crossed over the years. One little-known example comes in the form of David Williams – the long-established actor who was already on Equity's books when David tried to join the actors' union. Now in his late sixties, the original David Williams has been a professional entertainer for nearly 40 years – he got his first break on *Opportunity Knocks* when he performed a scene from *Oliver Twist* with a friend. Since then, he has played an extraordinary eight different characters in *Coronation Street*, two in *Emmerdale* and was in the original cast of *Brookside*. On the comedy front, he makes regular appearances in the Chuckle Brothers – and he reckons he would be a perfect fit for *Little Britain*. 'My favourite sketch is when David Walliams goes into the toyshop and the man behind the counter shouts out to his wife, "Margaret!" The man behind the counter looks like me and my wife is called Margaret,' he says.

Matt and David, who found out about the latter's namesake too late to include him in their latest series, are hoping to find a role for him in the future. 'I could play David's dad,' suggests the older man. Or, perhaps, his mum – for having played pantomime dames for years the older actor is just as ready to dress up as a lay-dee as his younger counterpart.

Another old-timer given a helping hand by the pair is Ted Robbins, the writer and performer who had been a big ITV star in Matt and David's childhoods. They refer to him constantly from *Rock Profile* onwards (including naming fictional bands after him) and ultimately employed him for cameo roles and as the warm-up man when *Little Britain* was being filmed.

Matt and David have also been generous enough to offer some support to the tribute act 'Littler Britain', which has sprung up to cash in on their fame. Many stars will go as far as to take legal action to try and ban these sort of unofficial enterprises. But Matt and David's view has been that, as long as fans aren't misled into thinking they are getting the real thing, there is no real problem with the lookalikes. 'I saw them on *Richard & Judy* and they seemed quite good,' said Matt, when he was asked about the young pretenders.

As their tour approached a natural break before the mammoth 35-date London residency in the autumn of 2006, Matt and David turned their thoughts to their comedy legacy. Both knew that time does funny things to the public's perception of comedians. If you are lucky as a performer, then your work is treated more kindly with every passing year – when people think back to the supposed golden age of comedy in the 1970s, for example, they think in generalities and don't analyse individual sketches as they do with today's shows. If you are less fortunate, however, your comedy is simply forgotten – seen as right for its time but wrong for posterity. Matt and David were determined to be in the former category, so they made plans to stay in the public eye with a Christmas special for the end of 2006. After all, two of their comedy heroes – Ronnie Corbett and Ronnie Barker – had done well enough out of the seasonal special route ('We're like Christmas lights – on the blink and only get turned on once a year,' was the way Ronnie Corbett had summed things up). Dawn French and Jennifer Saunders seemed equally keen on doing annual shows as a duo and a host of different projects as individuals throughout the rest of the year. If it worked for so many others, why not for Matt and David?

A slightly different take on the same subject came from long-time mentors Vic Reeves and Bob Mortimer. Their revival of existing characters in 2004's *Catterick* (in which Matt had a brilliant role as the hotelier-from-hell Mr Oates) showed one way in which you can extend a franchise beyond its original situation. Could Lou and Andy be given similar freedoms to star in a show of their own in 2007? That was one of the many joint projects the pair were working on as they sat in hotel rooms around the country during the national tour.

But, whatever they agree to do next, two things are clear. The first is that the men's extraordinary friendship will survive. Contrary to some expectations, Matt and David don't live in each other's pockets – they holiday and spend most evenings and weekends apart, for example. But, when they are together, they finish each other's sentences and subconsciously use the royal 'we' in almost every conversation. It is a relaxed, comfortable relationship, one that has been tested so much in the past that it is now entirely secure for the future.

The second guarantee is that their careers have equally strong foundations. *Little Britain* may or may not be on our screens in its existing format for much longer. But whether in terms of joint projects or individual achievements, it is clear that Matt Lucas and David Walliams are here to stay. More than 20 years have passed since the two suburban schoolboys sat at home doing impressions of their comedy heroes. Now millions of people have returned the favour by doing impressions of them. It has been both an incredible journey and an amazing achievement. And everyone who knows them says it's not over yet.